CONTENTS

Boston
Area by Area

Streetsmart

Within each Top 10 list in this book, no hierarchy of quality or popularity is implied. All 10 are, in the editor's opinion, of roughly equal merit.

Throughout this book, floors are referred to in accordance with American usage: i.e. the "first floor" is at ground level.

Front cover and spine *A picturesque view of Acorn Street, one of the narrow, cobblestoned-lanes of Beacon Hill*
Back cover *The Old State House in Downtown*
Title page *Federal-style facade of Massachusetts State House*

Welcome to
Boston

City of the future, cradle of American history. Hotbed of innovation, bastion of tradition. Like a polished gem cut from the rocky shores of New England, Boston has so many facets that discovering it can entertain visitors for days on end. It dazzles with renowned museums, great shopping, lush gardens and parks, and vibrant public spaces. With Eyewitness Top 10 Boston, it's yours to explore.

The fastest way to fall in love with Boston is to explore it on foot. Walk the **Freedom Trail** through the heart of Historic Downtown to famous Revolutionary War sites, including the **Paul Revere House**, **Old North Church**, and **Faneuil Hall**. From there you can explore the vibrant, green beauty of **Boston Common and Public Garden**; the majesty of **Trinity Church**, and the fun of high-fashion shopping along fabulous **Newbury Street**.

When you are ready for a taste of culture, what could be better than an evening listening to the fabled **Boston Pops Orchestra**, or a visit to the **Museum of Fine Arts**, or the delightfully eccentric **Isabella Stewart Gardner Museum**? And be sure to explore the remarkable science and art museums of **Harvard University**.

Did we mention the food? With the Atlantic Ocean as its front door and the farms of New England close by, it's no wonder that Boston is renowned for great seafood and farm-to-table-fresh fare, not to mention a wealth of delicious dishes from every part of the world.

Whether you're coming for a weekend or a week, our Top 10 guide brings together the best of everything the city can offer. It gives you tips throughout, from seeking out what's free to avoiding the crowds, plus 10 easy-to-follow itineraries, designed to help you visit a clutch of sights in a short space of time. Add inspiring photography and detailed maps, and you've got the essential pocket-sized travel companion. **Enjoy the book, and enjoy Boston**.

Clockwise from top: **Financial District from Boston Harbor, Federation-style rowhouses in Beacon Hill, Museum of Fine Arts, buoys in Rockport, Boston Public Garden in fall, cupola of Boston Custom House, Harvard University's Memorial Hall**

Exploring Boston

Whether you have just a couple of days, or more time to explore, there's so much to see and do in Boston. Here are some ideas for how to make the most of your time.

Boston Common is a vibrant green space in the heart of the city.

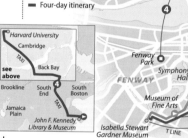

Key
— Two-day itinerary
— Four-day itinerary

Two Days in Boston

Day ❶
MORNING
Begin at **Boston Common and Public Garden** *(see pp18–19)*, and pick up a map for the **Freedom Trail** *(see pp12–15)* at the Information Kiosk. Walk the trail, stopping at **Faneuil Hall** *(see p13)* for lunch and to shop for souvenirs.
AFTERNOON
Continue along the Freedom Trail to the **Charlestown Navy Yard** *(see pp36–7)*, and then explore the **Museum of Science** *(see pp16–17)*. Pay a visit to **Harvard University** *(see pp20–23)* for a leisurely walk around campus and then take in a concert at **Sanders Theatre** *(see p61)*.

Day ❷
MORNING
Start off at the **Museum of Fine Arts** *(see pp28–31)* and then head off to **Newbury Street** *(see pp24–5)*, to enjoy the sights, shopping, and lunch.
AFTERNOON
Discover the Romanesque beauty of **Trinity Church** *(see pp32–3)* before exploring the exquisite collections of the **Isabella Stewart Gardner Museum** *(see pp34–5)*. In the evening, enjoy a show at the **Citi Performing Arts Center – Wang Theatre** *(see p60)*.

Four Days in Boston

Day ❶
MORNING
From **Boston Common and the Public Garden** *(see pp18–19)* explore **Beacon Hill** *(see pp80–85)* and the antiques shops of **Charles Street** *(see p84)*. Stop for lunch at **Artú** *(see p85)*.
AFTERNOON
Visit the **Isabella Stewart Gardner Museum** *(see pp34–5)* then dine at **Sorellina** *(see p93)* before a performance at **Symphony Hall** *(see p60)*.

Day ❷
MORNING
Explore **Back Bay** *(see pp86–93)*, visiting **Trinity Church** *(see pp32–3)*, the **Boston Public Library** *(see p87)*,

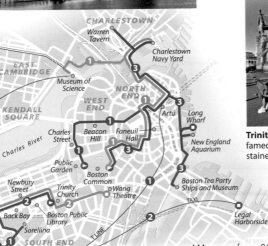

Boston Waterfront is a hub of history, as well as a venue for leisure and great seafood.

Trinity Church is famed for its beautiful stained glass.

and the art galleries and shops that make **Newbury Street** (see p91) a shopper's paradise.

AFTERNOON
Head to the **Museum of Fine Arts** (see pp28–31) for the afternoon, followed by a waterside seafood dinner at **Legal Harborside** (see p68).

Day ❸
MORNING
Walk the **Freedom Trail** (see pp12–15), pausing at **Faneuil Hall** (see p13) for coffee and a snack. At the end of the trail, tour the **Charlestown Navy Yard** (see pp36–7) and stop for lunch at the historic **Warren Tavern** (see p37).

AFTERNOON
Head over to the **New England Aquarium** (see pp38–9) and marvel at the marine life on display. Then take in the nearby **Boston Tea Party Ships**

and Museum (see p96), joining in with the revolutionary fun. Complete the day on a **Boston Harbor Cruises** (see p144) of Boston Harbor, departing from **Long Wharf** (see p46).

Day ❹
MORNING
Start at the **John F. Kennedy Library and Museum** (see p133) before heading to JFK's alma mater, **Harvard University** (see pp20–23), and exploring its campus.

AFTERNOON
After lunch in **Harvard Square** and a browse around its bookstores (see p75) visit the **Peabody and Natural History Museums** (see p123) and then head over to the fascinating **Museum of Science** (see p50). If the Red Sox are playing an evening game, head over to **Fenway Park** (see p117), but if you can't get hold of tickets, just make your way to **Game On!** (see p120), the on-site sports bar, and watch the game there.

Top 10 Boston Highlights

**Courtyard of the Isabella
Stewart Gardner Museum**

TOP 10 Boston Highlights

With its colonial-era architecture, lively seafaring heritage, and irrepressible Yankee character, Boston is one of the country's most distinctive locales. And, for all its big-city amenities – world-class restaurants, museums, and stores – visitors find it delightfully compact and walkable.

1 The Freedom Trail

Boston's best walking tour is free, self-guided, full of history, and open year round *(see pp12–15)*. It passes sights such as the Paul Revere House *(see p95)* where items including colonial banknotes can be seen.

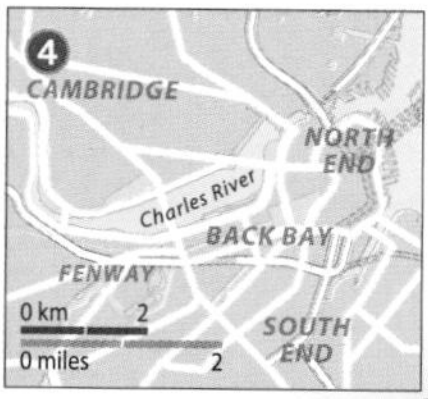

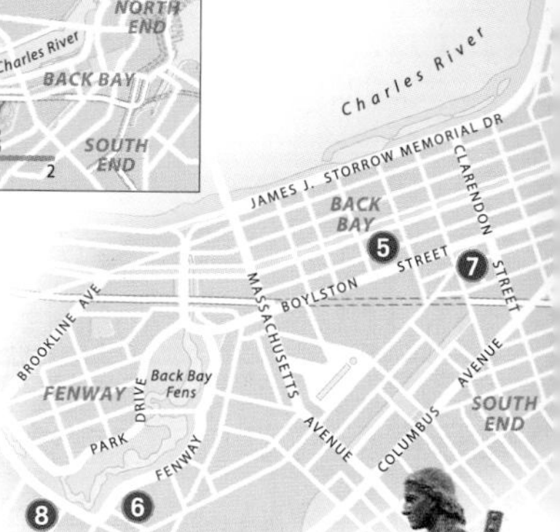

2 Museum of Science

One of Boston's liveliest and most-visited science museums, this remarkable facility delights with over 700 fascinating interactive exhibits *(see pp16–17)*.

3 Boston Common and Public Garden

Swan boats drift beneath weeping willows, children splash in fountains, and a bronzed George Washington oversees the proceedings from his lofty steed *(see pp18–19)*.

4 Harvard University

Established in 1636, the undisputed heart of American academia has cultivated some of the world's greatest thinkers and statesmen, including eight US presidents *(see pp20–23)*.

5 Around Newbury Street

Where fashionistas share the sidewalk with punk rockers. Nowhere are the city's myriad fashions, faces, and fortunes on more vibrant display *(see pp24–5)*.

6 Museum of Fine Arts, Boston

Boston's queen of the visual arts scene boasts some of the most extensive collections of Japanese, ancient Egyptian, and Impressionist works of art in the world *(see pp28–31)*.

7 Trinity Church

This Romanesque Revival church is considered the finest work by architect H. H. Richardson. Equally impressive is La Farge's *Christ in Majesty* window *(see pp32–3)*.

8 Isabella Stewart Gardner Museum

Masterpieces by the likes of Rembrandt, Botticelli, and Raphael appear all the more magnificent set in Isabella Stewart Gardner's Venetian-style palazzo built around a leafy courtyard *(see pp34–5)*.

9 Charlestown Navy Yard

Boston's deep harbor was ideal for one of the US Navy's first shipyards. The USS *Constitution*, built in 1797 (3 years prior to the Yard), is still docked here *(see pp36–7)*.

10 New England Aquarium

Get up close to four species of penguins, playful harbor seals, and myriad other creatures of the deep *(see pp38–9)*.

Map labels: WEST END · NORTH END · WATERFRONT · BEACON HILL · FINANCIAL DISTRICT · Puopolo Park · DOWNTOWN · Boston Common · CHARLES STREET · STUART STREET · CHINATOWN · 0 meters 500 · 0 yards 500

🔟⭐ The Freedom Trail

Snaking through 2.5 miles (4 km) of city streets, the Freedom Trail is a living link to Boston's key revolutionary and colonial-era sites. As you walk it, you'll see history adopt a vibrancy and palpability unparalleled among US cities. Some of Boston's most special stores, restaurants, and attractions are also located along the Trail.

① Massachusetts State House

Arguably Boston architect Charles Bulfinch's *pièce de résistance*, the "new" State House (completed in 1798) is one of the city's most distinctive buildings *(see pp15 & 81)*.

④ King's Chapel

The current granite building was erected in 1749, although the chapel was originally founded in 1686 by King James II as an outpost of the Anglican Church *(see p103)*. Don't miss the atmospheric burying ground next door, which shelters Massachusetts' first Governor, John Winthrop *(see p44)*.

⑥ Old State House

Built in 1713, this handsome colonial building **(left)** was the headquarters of the colonial legislature and the Royal Governor. The Declaration of Independence was first read from its balcony *(see p101)*.

② Park Street Church

Founded by a small group of Christians disenchanted with their Unitarian-leaning congregation, Park Street Church **(above)** was constructed in 1809.

⑤ Old South Meeting House

Boston's Old South Meeting House was, to the colonial era, a crucible for free-speech debates and protests against taxation *(see p102)*.

③ Old Granary Burying Ground

A veritable who's-who of revolutionary history fertilizes this plot **(right)** next to Park Street Church *(see p101)*. One of its most venerable residents is Samuel Adams *(see p44)*.

7 Faneuil Hall and Quincy Market

Known as the "Cradle of Liberty," Faneuil Hall has played host to many a revolutionary meeting in its time. Neighboring Quincy Market, built in the early 1800s, once housed Boston's wholesale food distribution *(see p101)*.

8 Paul Revere House

In North Square, the Paul Revere House **(above)** is Boston's oldest private residence. Its principal owner was well regarded locally as a metalsmith prior to his history-changing ride *(see p95)*.

AN HOUR OF FREEDOM

For visitors tight on time, consider this condensed trail. Head up Tremont Street from Park Street "T" station, stopping to visit the Old Granary Burying Ground. At the corner of Tremont and School streets – site of King's Chapel – turn right onto School and continue to Washington Street and the Old South Meeting House. Turn left on Washington to the Old State House then finish up at Faneuil Hall nearby on Congress Street.

9 Old North Church

This church **(below)** has a pivotal place in revolutionary history. Prior to his midnight ride, Revere *(see p44)* ordered Robert Newman to hang one or two lamps in the belfry to indicate, respectively, whether the British were approaching by land or via the Charles River *(see p95)*.

NEED TO KNOW

MAP P4 ■ Start point: Boston Common. "T" station: Park St (red/green lines) ■ Finish point: Charlestown. "T" station: Community College (orange line)

■ www.thefreedom trail.org

Copp's Hill Burying Ground: Hull St; 617 635 4505; open 9am–5pm daily; free

Park Street Church: 1 Park St; 617 523 3383 ■ www.parkstreet.org

■ Give your sweet tooth a workout at Mike's Pastry *(see p98)*.

■ Maps of the trail are available at the Boston Common Visitors' Center. Two-hour MP3 tours cost $15.

■ Most of the trail is indicated in red paint with a few sections in red brick.

10 Copp's Hill Burying Ground

With headstones dating from the 17th century, Copp's Hill is a must for history buffs. It was named after William Copp, a farmer who sold the land to the church *(see p95)*.

Moments in Revolutionary History

The Signing of the Declaration of Independence

1 Resistance to the Stamp Act (1765)

The king imposed a stamp duty on all published materials in the colonies, including newspapers. Furious Bostonians boycotted British goods in response.

2 Boston Massacre (1770)

Angry colonists picked a fight with British troops in front of the Old State House, resulting in the deaths of five unarmed Bostonians.

3 Samuel Adams' Tea Tax Speech (1773)

Adams' incendiary speech during a forum at the Old South Meeting House inspired the Boston Tea Party, the most subversive action undertaken yet in the debate over colonial secession.

4 Boston Tea Party (1773)

Led by Samuel Adams, the Sons of Liberty boarded three British East India Company ships and dumped their cargo into the Boston Harbor, a watershed moment of colonial defiance.

5 Paul Revere's Ride (1775)

Revere rode to Lexington to warn revolutionaries Samuel Adams and John Hancock that British troops intended to arrest them. One of the bravest acts of the war, it would be immortalized in the Longfellow poem *The Midnight Ride of Paul Revere*.

6 Battle of Lexington (1775)

Revere's ride was followed by the first exchange of fire between the ragtag colonist army and the British at Lexington.

7 Battle of Bunker Hill (1775)

The colonists' fortification of Charlestown resulted in a full-scale British attack. Despite their defeat, the colonists' resolve was galvanized by this battle.

8 Washington Takes Command (1776)

The Virginia gentleman farmer George Washington led the newly formed Continental Army south from Cambridge to face British troops in New York.

George Washington

9 Fortification of Dorchester Heights (1776)

Fortifying the mouth of Boston Harbor with captured cannon, George Washington put the Royal Navy under his guns and forced a British retreat from the city.

10 Declaration of Independence (1776)

On July 4, the colonies rejected all allegiance to the British Crown. Independence was declared from the Royal Governor's headquarters, the building known today as the Old State House (see p12).

MASSACHUSETTS STATE HOUSE

Finished in 1798, the State House is Charles Bulfinch's masterwork. With its brash design details, imposing stature, and liberal use of fine materials, it embodies the optimism of post-revolutionary America. The building is in three distinct sections: the original Bulfinch front; the marble wings constructed in 1917; and the yellow-brick 1895 addition, known as the Brigham Extension after the architect who designed it. Just below Bulfinch's central colonnade, statues of famous Massachusetts figures strike poses. Among them are the great orator Daniel Webster; President J. F. Kennedy; and Quaker Mary Dyer, who was hanged in 1660 for challenging the authority of Boston's religious leaders. Directly below the State House's immense gilded dome is the Senate Chamber, which has hosted some of the most influential debates and speeches in US history (see p81).

**TOP 10
STATE HOUSE
FEATURES**

1 23-carat gold dome

2 Senate Chamber

3 House of Representatives

4 "Hear Us" exhibit

5 Stained-glass windows

6 Doric Hall

7 Hall of Flags

8 Nurses Hall

9 Sacred Cod

10 State House Pine Cone

The Sacred Cod was bestowed on the House of Representatives by Boston merchant Jonathan Rowe. This carved fish has presided over the Commonwealth's legislature since 1784, though it vanished briefly in 1933, when Harvard's *Lampoon* magazine orchestrated a dastardly "codnapping" prank.

Facade of the Massachusetts State House

🔟 ⭐ Museum of Science

With over 700 colorful, interactive displays designed to thrill and expand the minds of kids and adults alike, it's little wonder that this is Boston's most-visited museum. Popular attractions include the jaw-dropping dome-shaped Imax screen in the **Mugar Omni Theater**, the new, techno-fabulous **Hall of Human Life**, the kid-pleasing lightning demonstrations, and daily live science shows.

5 Hall of Human Life

Visitors here are given an anonymous barcode wristband that is used to record their responses to the many challenges and activities on offer, and can then download their results and compare them to those of other visitors. Cutting-edge subjects are explored, such as DNA sequencing, GMO research and all sorts of medical and nutrition issues **(left)**.

1 To the Moon

This popular exhibit includes full-size replicas of the Apollo Command Module and the Lunar Module cockpit. Kids can climb into the pilots' seats and relive the first landing on the moon. Nearby models show the growth of space stations from Skylab and Mir to the International Space Station. Pieces of moon rock are on show as well.

2 Butterfly Garden

Visitors to this tropical greenhouse walk among clouds of brightly colored, fluttering butterflies from New England and around the world. Interactive displays and exhibits highlight fascinating butterfly facts including the four stages of a butterfly's life, plus the miracle of metamorphosis, and how they fly.

3 Colossal Fossil

Meet Cliff, one of only four nearly complete triceratops skeletons on display in the world. He looks pretty good for being 65 million years old. Discovered in North Dakota in 2004, Cliff measures 23 ft (7 m) from horn tip to tail, and his head alone weighs 800 lb (362 kg).

4 Children's Discovery Center

Geared to children under eight, this colorful, fun, activity-filled center is all about stimulating young minds with a sense of exploration. Kids can try their hands at being a Marine Biologist or a honey bee in a hive, or put an animal skeleton together. Friendly and well-trained staff help children discover the fun of problem-solving.

6 Thompson Theater of Electricity

This live-theater show explores the science of electricity. Its star is the world's largest Van de Graaff generator **(above)**, which safely zaps out sizzling lightning bolts of up to 1 million volts.

7 Charles Hayden Planetarium

This high-tech planetarium brings the dazzling night sky to life, and presents shows ranging from a look at NASA's latest space missions, to a kid-themed exploration of the stars with Sesame Street's Big Bird and Elmo.

Key to Floor Plan
- Second floor
- First floor
- Lower floor

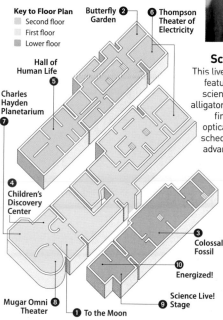

Butterfly **2** Garden

6 Thompson Theater of Electricity

Hall of Human Life **5**

Charles Hayden Planetarium **7**

4 Children's Discovery Center

Mugar Omni **8** Theater

1 To the Moon

Colossal **3** Fossil

10 Energized!

Science Live! **9** Stage

Science Live! Stage **9**

This live presentation **(above)** features mind-blowing hands-on science demonstrations. Meet an alligator, explore nanotechnology, or find out why our brains fall for optical illusions. A daily changing schedule keeps up with the latest advancements making the news.

10 Energized!

Innovative exhibits cover the latest in alternative energy, including solar, wind, and hydroelectric power, and the solutions they can offer.

8 Mugar Omni Theater

This remarkable IMax Theater takes the "big-screen" concept into a whole new realm. Visitors sit below a 180-degree dome that fills their entire range of vision, immersing their senses with spectacular sights and powerful digital sounds.

MUSEUM HISTORY

The Boston Museum of Science traces its origins back to the founding of the Boston Society of Natural History in 1830. The first permanent museum opened in 1864, making MOS one of the oldest science museums in America.

NEED TO KNOW

MAP G3 ■ 1 Science Park
■ 0123 456 789
■ www.mos.org
■ "T" station: Science Park (green line)

Open 9am–5pm Sat–Thu (Jul & Aug: to 7pm), 9am–9pm Fri

Adm: adults $23; seniors: $21; children (aged 3–11) $20

An extra fee is charged for admission to several attractions, including the Hayden Planetarium, the 4-D Theater, the Mugar Omni Theater and the Butterfly Garden. Individual admission to these attractions ranges from $4 to $10. The "Add More, Spend Less!" program offers admission to all four

of these attractions for a flat rate of $6.

■ The museum's Riverview Café (level 1, by the Museum Store) features several food stations, including a taqueria, Puck's (light meals designed by celebrity chef Wolfgang Puck), a burger grill, salad bar, sandwich stand, and a Starbucks coffee shop.

⭐ Boston Common and Public Garden

Verdant Boston Common has hosted auctions, cattle grazing, and public hangings over its 380-year history, in addition to festivals and the requisite frisbee tosses. The adjacent Public Garden, opened in 1839, was the US's first botanical garden. Its swan boats and weeping willows are emblematic of Boston at its most enchanting. The French-style flowerbeds may only bloom in warmer months, but the garden exudes old-world charm year round.

1 Frog Pond

During summer, children splash under the iridescent spray of the pond's fountains (**above**). Come winter, kids of all ages lace up their skates and take to the ice. Skate rentals and delicious hot chocolate are nearby.

2 Lagoon Bridge

This elegant 1869 bridge that spans over the lagoon is a National Historic Landmark, and is a favorite spot for wedding pictures.

3 Make Way for Ducklings Statuettes

Eight little ducklings seem to have sprung from the pages of Robert McCloskey's much-loved kids' book and fallen in line behind their mother at the lagoon's edge (**right**).

4 Shaw Memorial

Augustus Saint-Gaudens' lifelike bronze pays homage to the "Fighting 54th" – one of the only entirely African-American regiments in the Civil War. Led by Boston native Robert Shaw, the 54th amassed an impressive battle record.

5 Bronze of George Washington

The nation's first president cuts a stately figure at the western end of the Public Garden (**above**). Local sculptor Thomas Ball's 1869 bronze was the first to show Washington astride a horse.

6 Soldiers and Sailors Monument

Over 25,000 Union Army veterans remembered their fallen Civil War comrades at the 1877 dedication of Martin Milmore's impressive memorial. Bas-reliefs depict the soldiers' and sailors' departure to and return from war.

Plan of Boston Common and Public Garden

7 Founders' Memorial

William Blaxton, Boston's first white settler, is depicted greeting John Winthrop *(see p44)* in John F. Paramino's 1930 bronze. Note the use of the word "Shawmut" – the Native American name for the land that would become Boston.

8 Swan Boats

Summer hasn't officially arrived in Boston until the swan boats emerge from hibernation and glide onto the Public Garden lagoon. With their gracefully arching necks and brilliantly painted bills, each distinctive swan can accommodate up to 20 people.

9 Parkman Bandstand

Built in 1912 to honor George Parkman, a bene-factor of the park, this elegant bandstand **(left)** is modeled on Versailles' *Temple d'Amour* (temple of love). In summer it hosts everything from concerts to graduations.

10 Ether Monument

This 1868 statue commemorates the first ether-ized operation, which took place at Massachusetts General Hospital in 1846 *(see p49)*. Controversial from the outset, this is the West's only monument to the powers of a drug.

EMERALD NECKLACE

Boston Common and Public Garden may seem like solitary urban oases, but they are two links in a greater chain of green space that stretches all the way through Boston to the suburb of Roxbury. The Emerald Necklace, as this chain is called, was completed in 1896 by Frederick Law Olmsted, the man behind New York's Central Park.

NEED TO KNOW

MAP M4, N4
■ Bounded by: Beacon, Park, Tremont, Arlington, & Boylston streets
■ "T" station: Park Street (red/green line), Boylston & Arlington (both green line)

Open 24 hours

Boston Common Visitors' Center: 139 Tremont St; 617 426 3115; open 8:30am–5pm Mon–Fri, 9am–5pm Sat & Sun

Boston Parks & Recreation: 617 635 2090; www.cityofboston. gov/parks ■ Swan boat rides: 617 522 1966; mid-Apr–mid-Sep: usually 10am–5pm daily; Adm: $3; www.swanboats.com

■ Quick, food court-style bites can be had inside the Corner shopping center, at Washington and Summer streets.

■ The Commonwealth Shakespeare Company stages free perform-ances during summer. Contact 617 426 0863 or check the website www.commshakes.org

🔟 ⭐ Harvard University

America's most prestigious university – named for its earliest benefactor, John Harvard, in 1638 – has nurtured, tortured, and tickled some of the greatest minds of the past 380 years. It has hosted everything from global economic summits to kool-aid acid tests, and educated everyone from future US presidents to talk-show hosts. Visitors craving contact with the Harvard mystique are in luck – much of the university is open to the public.

1 Massachusetts Hall

The university's oldest building, constructed in 1720, was a barrack for 640 revolutionary soldiers. It continues to be a focal point of protest – in 2015, Heat Week saw a blockade against fossil fuel endowments made to the university.

2 John Harvard Statue

The inscription "John Harvard, Founder 1638" conceals three deceptions, hence its nickname "The Statue of Three Lies." First, there is no known portrait of John Harvard, so the sculptor used a model; second, Harvard did not found the university – it was named after him; and last, it was founded in 1636, not 1638.

3 Memorial Hall

Built over 14 years, Harvard's memorial to its fallen Union army alumni was officially opened in 1878. Conceived as a multipurpose building, it has hosted graduation exercises, theatrical performances, and assemblies of many other kinds **(above)**.

5 Harvard Yard

Harvard's mixed residential and academic yard became the standard by which most American institutions of higher learning modeled their campuses.

6 Harry Widener Memorial Library

The Widener is the largest university library in the US. It houses an extremely impressive collection of rare books, including a Gutenberg Bible and early editions of Shakespeare's collected works.

4 Museum of Natural History

Never mind George Washington's taxidermied pheasants, the enormous Brazilian amethyst geode, or the world's only mounted Kronosaurus skeleton; check out the glass flowers: 830 species of plants, painstakingly replicated in colorful glass **(above)**.

7 Harvard Art Museums

Harvard's art collections were brought under one roof in a Renzo Piano building in 2014. It displays works from Fogg Museum's world-class collection of European and American art **(above)**, Germanic art holdings of the Busch-Reisinger Museum, and Asian collections of the Sackler Museum.

8 Science Center Plaza

This plaza in front of the Undergraduate Science Center is Harvard's busiest social space, featuring the Tanner Fountain, cafés, and food trucks.

9 Semitic Museum

Founded in 1889, this museum houses more than 40,000 objects from excavations in Egypt, Iraq, Israel, Jordan, Syria, and Tunisia.

10 Peabody Museum of Archaeology and Ethnology

One of the world's most comprehensive records of human cultural history, the Peabody caters for the Indiana Jones in all of us. Highlights include The Hall of the North American Indian **(below)**, a permanent Mesoamerica exhibit, and a gallery devoted to rotating temporary exhibits.

HARVARD LAMPOON

Lampooners have made you laugh more than you might ever know. Aside from *The Harvard Lampoon* proper being the world's oldest humor magazine, nearly every successful contemporary American comedy to reach a television or movie screen boasts an ex-Lampooner on its writing staff. Well-known ex-Lampooners include the popular late-night TV host Conan O'Brien.

NEED TO KNOW

MAP B1–C1 ■ "T" station: Harvard (red line) ■ www.harvard. edu; www.cambridge-usa.org

Harry Widener Memorial Library: Harvard Yard; 617 495 2411; access only if accompanied by someone with valid Harvard ID

Maps and campus tours available from Holyoke Center: 1350 Massachusetts Ave; 617 495 1573

■ Students refuel at the Harvard Coop bookstore café (1400 Massachusetts Ave, 617 499 2000).

■ Harvard Film Archive, Carpenter Center, screens art and documentary films most nights (24 Quincy St, 617 495 4700).

■ Pick up a copy of the student-run newspaper *The Crimson* to see what current issues are exercising some of the world's greatest minds.

Harvard Alumni

1 John Adams (1735–1826)
The nation's second president, although nervous upon entering the illustrious college as a freshman, eventually became enthralled by his studies.

2 Franklin Delano Roosevelt (1882–1945)
Apparently more of a social butterfly than a dedicated academic, F.D.R. played pranks, led the freshman football squad, edited the *Harvard Crimson*, and earned a C average at Harvard before going on to become the 32nd President of the US.

3 W. E. B. Du Bois (1868–1963)
Founder of the National Association for the Advancement of Colored People (NAACP), Du Bois studied philosophy here, and said of his experience, "I was in Harvard, but not of it."

4 J. F. Kennedy (1917–63)
A barely average student, but a good athlete, John F. Kennedy ran for President of the Freshman Class in 1936, and lost badly. He did rather better in 1960 when he became the 35th President of the United States.

Barack Obama

5 Barack Obama (1961–)
The 44th President of the United States attended Harvard Law School from 1988–91. His election as the first black president of the Harvard Law Review gained extensive media attention.

6 Leonard Bernstein (1918–90)
The country's greatest composer and conductor was firmly grounded in the arts at Harvard. He edited the *Advocate* – the college's estimable literary and performing arts journal.

Leonard Bernstein

7 T. S. Eliot (1885–1965)
The modernist poet of *The Waste Land* fame contributed much of his early work to the *Advocate*. He went on to edit many of those submissions for later publication.

8 Henry Kissinger (1923–)
The International Affairs and Government professor, who graduated from Harvard *summa cum laude* (with highest distinction), became President Nixon's National Security Advisor in 1969 and Secretary of State in 1973.

9 Benazir Bhutto (1953–2007)
This class of 1973 alumna later became the first woman to lead a modern Muslim state when she was elected prime minister of Pakistan in 1988. She was assassinated in 2007.

10 Henry James (1843–1916)
The master of the psychological novel sourced plenty of material at Harvard for his scathing 1886 work *The Bostonians*.

HARVARD'S "ARCHITECTURAL ZOO"

Prominent modernist architect James Stirling described Harvard as an "architectural zoo" – and it's a well-deserved moniker. Stirling was responsible for the university's modernist 1985 Sackler Museum building *(see p21 & p123)* that now houses offices. Charles Bulfinch, whose claim to fame is the Massachusetts State House *(see p12)*, contributed the 1814 University Hall, featuring an ingenious granite staircase that "floats" – supported solely by virtue of its inter-locking steps. In contrast, Walter Gropius, whose strongly linear residential buildings pepper college campuses throughout the northeast US, designed the Harvard Graduate Center in 1950. He strove to make his industry-informed projects seem welcoming for their inhabitants, but by most Harvard grad students' accounts, it doesn't exactly scream "home sweet home." Le Corbusier's Carpenter Center is a wondrous collection of forms and materials. The center boasts entire walls made of glass and deeply grooved concrete. Perhaps surprisingly, it is Le Corbusier's only design in North America.

TOP 10
HARVARD'S BUILDINGS

1 Memorial Hall, 45 Quincy St (Ware and Van Brunt, 1878)

2 Loeb Drama Center, 64 Brattle St (Hugh Stebbins, 1959)

3 Massachusetts Hall, Harvard Yard (University Overseers, 1720)

4 Sackler Museum building, 485 Broadway (James Stirling, 1985)

5 Harvard Art Museums, 32 Quincy Street (Renzo Piano and Payette, 2014)

6 University Hall, Harvard Yard (Charles Bulfinch, 1814)

7 Sever and Austin halls, Harvard Yard and North Yard (H. H. Richardson, 1880 and 1883)

8 Harvard Graduate Center, North Yard (Walter Gropius, 1950)

9 Carpenter Center, 24 Quincy St (Le Corbusier, 1963)

10 Undergraduate Science Center, Oxford St (Josep Lluís Sert, 1971)

Sever Hall and Austin Hall were designed by architect and 1859 Harvard alumnus H. H. Richardson. Both halls echo the distinctive Romanesque style found on his Copley Square masterpiece – Trinity Church *(see pp32–3)*.

Carpenter Center for Visual Arts, designed by Le Corbusier

🔟 ⭐ Around Newbury Street

Don't let the profusion of Prada-clad shoppers fool you: there's much more to elegant Newbury Street than world-class retail, people-watching, and alfresco dining. One of the first streets created on the marshland once known as Back Bay, Newbury has seen myriad tenants and uses over the past 150 years. Look closely and you'll glimpse a historical side to Newbury Street all but unseen by the fashionistas.

3 Church of the Covenant

Although far more famous for his Trinity Church in New York, English-born architect Richard Upjohn also left his Neo-Gothic mark on Boston with the Church of the Covenant **(left)**, erected in 1865.

4 Society of Arts and Crafts

Formed in 1897, the Boston Society of Arts and Crafts was one of the earliest of its kind. Societies such as this helped to elevate the status of traditional arts (see p90).

1 Emmanuel Church

Architect Alexander Estey's impressive church (1860) was the first building to grace Newbury after the infilling of Back Bay. The adjacent Lindsey Chapel (1924) is home to the renowned Emmanuel Music ensemble.

2 French Cultural Center

Housed in a grand Back Bay mansion, the French Cultural Center hosts everything from lectures in French to concerts and a tasteful Bastille Day celebration. It also runs summer courses in French for all ages.

5 New England Historic Genealogical Society

Members seek to discover more about their New England progenitors in one of the most extensive genealogical libraries in the US.

6 234 Berkeley St

Originally a natural history museum opened in 1864, this landmark building is now a high-end home goods store.

7 Commonwealth Avenue

A mall running along the center of Commonwealth Avenue provides a leafy respite from the Newbury Street throngs. Benches and historical sculptures **(left)**, line the pedestrian path (see p88).

⑧ Gibson House Museum

One of Back Bay's first private homes, Gibson House **(left)** was also one of the most modern residences of its day. With its gas lighting, indoor plumbing, and heating, it spurred a building boom in the area *(see p88)*.

BACK BAY'S ORIGINS

Since its settlement by Europeans, Boston has been reshaped to suit the needs of its inhabitants. Back Bay derives its name from the tidal swampland on which the neighborhood now stands. During the 19th century, gravel was used to fill the marsh and create the foundations for the grand avenues and picturesque brownstone buildings that now distinguish this sought-after area.

Newbury Street

⑨ Boston Architectural College

For more than 120 years, aspiring architects have studied at this college **(below)**. The McCormick Gallery has architectural plans and designs.

⑩ Trinity Church Rectory

H. H. Richardson, Trinity Church's principal architect, was commissioned to build this rectory in 1879. His handiwork echoes the Romanesque style of the church itself on Copley Square *(see pp32–3)*.

NEED TO KNOW

MAP K5, L5, M5 ■ "T" station: Arlington, Copley, or Hynes/ICA

Boston Architectural College: 320 Newbury St; 617 585 0100; open 8:30am–10pm Mon–Thu, 9am–9pm Fri, 9am–5pm Sat, noon–7pm Sun

Church of the Covenant: 67 Newbury St

Emmanuel Church: 15 Newbury St

French Cultural Center: 53 Marlborough St; 617 912 0400; open 10am–5pm Mon–Thu & Sat, later hours some evenings

New England Historic Genealogical Society: 101 Newbury St; 617 536 5740; open 9am–5pm Tue–Sat (until 9pm Wed)

Society of Arts and Crafts: 175 Newbury St; 617 266 1810; open 10am–6pm Tue–Sat

Trinity Church Rectory: 233 Clarendon St; not open to the public

■ Buy picnic supplies at Deluca's Back Bay Market (239 Newbury St).

■ View the schedule for Emmanuel Music at www.emmanuelmusic.org

Following pages Aerial view of Boston Harbor

TOP 10 ⭐ Museum of Fine Arts, Boston

Over its 140-year-plus history, the MFA has collected some 450,000 pieces from an array of cultures and civilizations, ranging from ancient Egyptian tomb treasures to stylish modern artworks. In 2010, the museum opened its long-anticipated Art of the Americas wing, designed by Norman Foster, which displays works created in North, Central, and South America.

4 Sargent Murals

Having secured some of John Singer Sargent's most important portraiture in the early 20th century, the MFA went one step further and commissioned the artist to paint murals and bas-reliefs on its central rotunda and colonnade. They feature gods and heroes from classical mythology.

1 Postman Joseph Roulin

The MFA houses some of Vincent van Gogh's most important works, including this 1888 portrait, which was painted during his stay in Arles, France.

3 Egyptian Royal Pectoral

This extremely rare chest ornament (above) is nearly 4,000 years old. A vulture is depicted with a cobra on its left wing, poised to strike.

5 Dance at Bougival

This endearing image (1883) of a young couple dancing is one of the most beloved of Renoir's works. It exemplifies the artist's knack for taking a timeless situation and making it contemporary by dressing his subjects in the latest fashions.

6 Silverwork by Paul Revere

Famed for his midnight ride, Revere (see p44) was also known for his masterful silverwork (left). The breadth of his ability is apparent in the museum's magnificent 200-piece collection.

John Singleton Copley Portraits 2

Self-taught, Boston-born Copley made a name for himself by painting the most affluent and influential Bostonians of his day (right), from pre-revolutionary figures like John Hancock to early American presidents such as John Quincy Adams.

8 La Japonaise
Claude Monet's 1876 portrait **(left)** reflects a time when Japanese culture fascinated Europe's most style-conscious circles. The model, interestingly, is Monet's wife, Camille.

9 Japanese Temple Room
With its wood paneling and subdued lighting, the Temple Room evokes ancient Japanese shrines atop mist-enshrouded mountains. The statues, which date from as early as the 7th century, depict prominent figures from Buddhist texts.

10 Statue of King Aspelta
This statue **(right)** of the 6th-century BC Nubian king, Aspelta, was recovered in 1920 at Nuri in present-day Sudan during a Museum of Fine Arts/ Harvard joint expedition.

7 Christ in Majesty with Symbols
Acquired in 1919 from a small Spanish church, this medieval fresco had an amazingly complex journey to Boston, which involved waterproofing it with lime and Parmesan for safe transportation.

NEED TO KNOW

MAP D6 ■ 465 Huntington Ave (Ave of the Arts) ■ 617 267 9300 ■ www.mfa.org ■ "T" station: Museum (green line/E train)

Open 10am–4:45pm Mon & Tue, 10am–9:45pm Wed– Fri, 10am–4:45pm Sat & Sun

Adm: $23–$25

■ The MFA has four restaurants and cafés, escalating in quality and price as you move from the courtyard level upward.

■ The MFA's Family Art Cart in the Shapiro Family Courtyard provides activities and materials to use in the galleries. Consult the museum's website for a full schedule of events.

■ Admission to the museum on Wednesdays 4–9:45pm is by voluntary donation.

Gallery Guide
European, Classical, Far Eastern, and Egyptian art and artifacts occupy the original MFA building.

The informative Visitor Center is located on Level 1. The Linde Wing for Contemporary Art, on the west side of the museum, also houses the museum shop, cafés, and a restaurant. Arts from the Americas are spread across four levels in the Art of the Americas wing, on the east side of the museum. The wing has 53 galleries, plus a state-of-the-art auditorium, and displays over 5,000 works of art.

Museum of Fine Arts Collections

Art of Asia

For Asian art connoisseurs, the museum offers a dizzying overview of Japan's multiple artistic forms. In fact, the MFA holds the largest collection of ancient Japanese art outside of Japan. In addition to the tranquil Temple Room *(see p29)*, with its centuries-old Buddhist statues, visitors should look out for the beautiful hanging scrolls and woodblock prints, with their magical, dramatic landscapes and spirited renderings of everyday life. Kurasawa fans, meanwhile, will be enthralled by the menacing samurai weaponry. Additionally, the Art of Asia collection contains exquisite objects from 2,000 years of Chinese, Indian, and Southeast Asian history, including sensuous ivory figurines, pictorial carpets, and vibrant watercolors.

Stuart woman's doublet, dating from 1610–15

Textile and Fashion Arts

Rotating displays highlight pictorial quilts, period fashions, fine Persian rugs, and pre-colonial Andean weavings. Particularly interesting are the textiles and costumes from the Elizabethan and Stuart periods – an unprecedented 1943 donation from the private collection of Elizabeth Day McCormick.

Classical Art

The remarkable Classical Art Collection has a hoard of gold bracelets, glass, mosaic bowls, and stately marble busts. One of the earliest pieces is a c.1500 BC gold axe, inscribed with symbols from a still-undeciphered Cretan language

Art of the Americas

The MFA's Art of the Americas wing, designed by Norman Foster, opened in 2010. The wing features pieces dating from pre-Columbian times, through to the third quarter of the 20th century, and showcases about 5,000 works produced in North, Central, and South America. The museum has profited from generous benefactors over the years and the collection holds the world's finest ensemble of colonial New England furniture, rare 17th-century American portraiture, a superb display of American silver, and paintings by the country's own "Old" Masters, including Copley, Stuart, Cole, Sargent, Cassat, Homer, and many others.

Art of Egypt, Nubia, and the Ancient Near East

This collection is a treasure trove of millennia-old Egyptian sarcophagi, tomb finds, and Nubian jewelry and

Japan "Golden Age" (1781–1801) print

Egyptian mummy mask (AD 1–50)

objects from everyday life. The assemblage of Egyptian funerary pieces, including beautifully crafted jewelry and ceramic urns, is quite awe-inspiring. Ancient Near Eastern objects, with their bold iconography and rich materials, illustrate why the region is known as one of the Cradles of Civilization.

6 European Art to 1900

From 12th-century tempera baptism scenes to Claude Monet's *Haystacks*, the MFA's European collection is staggeringly diverse. Painstakingly transferred medieval stained-glass windows, beautifully illuminated bibles, and delicate French tapestries are displayed alongside works by Old Masters: Titian, El Greco, Rembrandt, and Rubens. A superlative Impressionist and Post-Impressionist collection boasts masterpieces from the likes of Renoir, Degas, Cézanne, and Van Gogh, plus the finest group of Monet's works outside of Paris.

La Berceuse (1889) by Van Gogh

7 Contemporary Art

Given Boston's affinity for the traditional, you might be surprised by this world-class collection of contemporary and late 20th-century art. It includes works by the painter and photographer Chuck Close and the abstract Expressionist artist Jackson Pollock, which are on display in the Art of the Americas wing. New Media is also well represented here.

Tibetan conch shell trumpet

8 Musical Instruments

Priceless 17th-century guitars, ornately inlaid pianos, and even a mouth organ are on view to visitors of the MFA. Among the more distinctive pieces is a c.1796 English grand piano – the earliest extant example of a piano with a six-octave range – and a 1680 French guitar by the Voboam workshop.

9 Art of Africa and Oceania

Pre-colonial artifacts from these collections include Melanese canoe ornaments, dramatic Congolese bird sculptures and African funerary art. The most popular African display is the powerful-looking 19th- and 20th-century wooden masks.

10 "Please be Seated!" Installations

View (and sit on) one of the country's most comprehensive collections of American contemporary furniture. The museum encourages visitors to admire and sit on these furniture pieces. Take a break and have a seat on fine American handiwork by designers such as Maloof, Castle, and Eames.

TOP10 ⭐ Trinity Church

Boston has a great knack for creating curious visual juxtapositions, and one of the most remarkable is in Copley Square, where Henry Hobson Richardson's 19th-century Romanesque Trinity Church reflects in the sleek, blue-tinted glass of the decidedly 20th-century 200 Clarendon Tower nearby. The breathtakingly beautiful church was named a National Historic Landmark in 1971 and has earned the distinction of being listed among the American Institute of Architects' ten greatest buildings in the country.

Burne-Jones Windows ①

Edward Burne-Jones' windows **(right)** – on the Boylston Street side – were inspired by the burgeoning English Arts and Crafts Movement. Its influence is readily apparent in his *David's Charge to Solomon*, with its bold patterning and rich colors.

② The Foundation

As part of Richardson's daring plan, the first of 4,500 wooden support pilings for the church was driven into the soggy Back Bay landfill in 1873. Reverend Phillips Brooks laid the cornerstone two years later.

③ Central Tower

The church's central tower borrows its square design from the Cathedral of Salamanca, Spain. On the interior, wall paintings by La Farge depicting biblical figures in vibrant hues are in sharp contrast to the normally austere church interiors of the artist's day.

④ Front Facade and Side Towers

The Romanesque church of St Trophime in Arles, France, was the inspiration when Richardson redesigned Trinity's front portico, along with its two new side towers **(left)**. The additions were put in place by his firm of architects in the 1890s, after his death in 1886.

Interior of Trinity Church

⑤ Embroidered Kneelers

Trinity's colorful kneelers have been stitched by parishioners in memory of people and events past. They serve as an informal folk history of the congregation.

⑥ Pulpit Carving

Preachers from throughout the ages, including St. Paul, Martin Luther, and Phillips Brooks of Trinity, are depicted in high relief on the pulpit designed by Charles Coolidge.

Phillips Brooks' Bust ⑦
Keeping watch over the baptismal font is Rector Brooks **(right)**. Renowned for his bold, original sermons, he was rector at Trinity from 1869–91.

⑧ The Shop at Trinity
As well as religious books and items, the store also sells works by local artists and CDs of Trinity Choir.

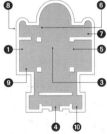

TRINITY SINGS "HALLELUJAH"

One of Boston's most cherished traditions is the singing of Handel's *Messiah*, with its rousing and unmistakable "Hallelujah Chorus," at Trinity during the Christmas season. Hundreds pack the sanctuary to experience the choir's ethereal, masterful treatment of the piece. Call 617 536 0944 for performance information.

⑩ Organ Pipes
The beautiful organ pipes frame the church's west wall. Exquisitely designed, ornately painted, and – of course – extremely sonorous, the pipes seem to hug the church's ceiling arches.

Church Floor Plan

⑨ La Farge Windows
A newcomer to stained glasswork at the time, John La Farge approached his commissions, such as the breathtaking *Christ in Majesty*, with the same sense of daring and vitality that architect Richardson employed in his Trinity design.

NEED TO KNOW

MAP L5 ■ 206 Clarendon St ■ "T" station: Copley Sq (green line) & Back Bay (orange line) ■ 617 536 0944 (church) ■ www.trinitychurchboston.org

Church open for self-guided tours: 9am–4:45pm Mon–Sat, 11:15am–5:45pm Sun

Shop open 9am–5pm Mon–Sat, 10am–6pm Sun

Guided tours: $7

■ Grab a quick bite at the Prudential Center food court, just two blocks away (800 Boylston St).

■ From September to June organ recitals are held every Friday,

12:15–12:45pm. By donation.

■ Guided tours of the church are available and begin in the Shop at Trinity on the Boylston Street side of the complex.

■ In summer, a free guided tour is offered every Sunday following the 10am service.

🔟⭐ Isabella Stewart Gardner Museum

One needn't be a patron of the arts to be wowed by the Gardner Museum. Its namesake traveled tirelessly to acquire a world-class art collection, which is housed in a Venetian-style palazzo where flowers bloom, sculpted nudes pose in hidden corners, and entire ceilings reveal their European origins. The palace is complemented by a striking modern building, designed by Renzo Piano, which holds an intimate performance hall, galleries, and a charming café.

1 Titian Room
The most artistically significant gallery was conceived by Gardner as the palazzo's grand reception hall. It has an Italian flavor and showcases Cillini's *Bindo Altoviti* **(left)** and Titian's *Europa*, one of the best masterpieces in the US.

2 The Courtyard
Gardner integrated Roman, Byzantine, Romanesque, Renaissance, and Gothic elements in the magnificent courtyard **(right)**, which is out of bounds but can be viewed through the graceful arches surrounding it.

3 Long Gallery
Roman sculptural fragments and busts line glass cases crammed with unusual 15th- and 16th-century books and artifacts. One such rare tome is a 1481 copy of Dante's *The Divine Comedy*, which features drawings by Botticelli.

4 Tapestry Room
Restored to its original 1914 state, this sweeping gallery houses two 16th-century Belgian tapestry cycles: one depicting *Scenes from the Life of Cyrus the Great* and the other *Scenes from the Life of Abraham*.

5 Dutch Room
Housing some of Gardner's most impressive acquisitions, this was the scene of an incredible art heist in 1990: among the 13 works stolen were a Vermeer and two Rembrandts.

6 Macknight, Yellow, and Blue Rooms
Fans of Impressionism will love the Macknight, Yellow and Blue **(left)** rooms, which house portraits and sketches by Manet, Matisse, Degas, and Sargent. Of particular note is Sargent's *Mrs Gardner in White*.

7 Gothic Room
John Singer Sargent's grand and somewhat risqué 1888 portrait of Mrs Gardner is here **(left)**, as well as medieval liturgical artwork from the 13th century.

8 Veronese Room
With its richly gilded and painted Spanish-leather wall-coverings, it's easy to miss this gallery's highlight: look up at Paolo Veronese's 16th-century master-work *The Coronation of Hebe*.

FENWAY COURT

Before Isabella Stewart Gardner died in 1924 she stipulated in her will that her home and her collection become a public museum. She believed that works of art should be displayed in a setting that would fire the imagination. So the collection, exhibited over three floors, is arranged purely to enhance the viewing of the individual treasures. To encourage visitors to respond to the artworks themselves, many of the 2,500 objects – from ancient Egyptian pieces to Matisse's paintings – are left unlabeled, as Gardner had requested.

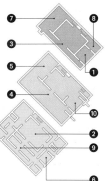

Key to Floor Plan
- First floor
- Second floor
- Third floor

NEED TO KNOW

MAP D6 ■ 280 The Fenway ■ 617 566 1401 ■ www.gardner museum.org ■ "T" station: Museum (green line/E train)

Open 11am–5pm Wed–Mon (to 9pm Thu) ■ Adm: $12–$15; free to anyone named Isabella

■ Light salads and sandwiches are served in the museum's café. Weather permitting, request a table outdoors in the garden.

■ The museum's Calderwood Hall hosts a concert series in the spring and fall. See museum website.

■ Gardner After Hours, on the third Thursday of each month, hosts live jazz, a wine bar, and games late into the evening.

9 Spanish Cloister
With stunning mosaic tiling and a Moorish arch, the Spanish Cloister looks like a hidden patio at the Alhambra. But Sargent's sweeping *El Jaleo* (1882), all sultry shadows and rich hues, gives the room its distinctiveness.

10 Raphael Room
Gardner was the first collector to bring works by Raphael to the US; three of his major works are on display here, alongside Botticelli's *Tragedy of Lucretia* and Crivelli's *St. George and the Dragon*.

Charlestown Navy Yard

Some of the most storied battleships in American naval history began life at Charlestown Navy Yard. Established in 1800 as one of the country's first naval yards, Charlestown remained vital to US security until its decommissioning in 1974. From the wooden-hulled USS *Constitution* built in 1797 to the World War II steel destroyer USS *Cassin Young*, the yard gives visitors an all-hands-on-deck historical experience unparalleled in America.

1 USS Constitution

First tested in action during the War of 1812, the USS *Constitution* (above) is the world's oldest warship still afloat. A tugboat helps her perform an annual turnaround cruise on July 4th.

2 Navy Yard Visitor Center

Begin your stroll through the yard at the National Park Service-operated Visitor Center, where you can pick up literature about the site's many attractions and check on tour schedules.

3 Bunker Hill Monument

This 220-ft (67-m) granite obelisk (right), near the yard, has towered over Charlestown since 1842. It was built to commemorate the first major battle of the American Revolution (see p14).

4 USS Cassin Young

Never defeated, despite withstanding multiple kamikaze bomber-attacks in the Pacific, this World War II era destroyer (right) could be considered USS *Constitution's* 20th-century successor.

5 Commandant's House

The oldest building in the yard, dating from 1805, housed the commandants of the First Naval District. With its sweeping harbor views and wrap-around veranda, this elegant mansion was ideal for entertaining dignitaries from all over the world.

6 Dry Dock #1

To facilitate hull repairs, Dry Dock #1 **(left)** was opened in 1833. It was drained by massive steam-powered pumps. USS *Constitution* was the first ship to be given an overhaul here.

7 Ropewalk

This quarter-mile-long (0.5 km) building (1837) houses steam-powered machinery that produced rope rigging for the nation's warships.

8 USS Constitution Museum

With activities to keep kids entertained, as well as enough nautical trivia and artifacts **(above)** – from muskets to spoils of war – to satisfy a naval historian, this museum brings to life USS *Constitution's* two centuries of service.

9 Muster House

This octagonal brick building was designed in the Georgian-revival style popular in the northeast in the mid 19th century. The house served as an administration hub, where the yard's clerical work was carried out.

Charlestown Navy Yard

10 Marine Railway

The Navy Yard has constantly evolved to meet changing demands and developments. The marine railway was built in 1918 to haul submarines and other vessels out of the water for hull repairs.

OLD IRONSIDES

Given her 25-inch (63-cm) thick hull at the waterline, it's easy to imagine why USS *Constitution* earned her nickname "Old Ironsides." Pitted against HMS *Guerriere* during the War of 1812, the ship engaged in a shoot-out that left *Guerriere* all but destroyed. Seeing British cannon balls "bouncing" off USS *Constitution's* hull, a sailor allegedly exclaimed, "Huzzah! Her sides are made of iron." The rest is history.

NEED TO KNOW

MAP H2 ▪ Visitor Center: Building Number 5 ▪ 617 242 5601 ▪ www. nps.gov/bost ▪ "T" station: North Station (green & orange lines) ▪ Water shuttle from Long Wharf, www. mbta.com

Bunker Hill Monument: open 9am–5pm daily; last climb 4:30pm

Naval Yard Visitor Center: open 9am–5pm daily

USS Cassin Young: open 10am–4pm daily
USS Constitution: open 10am–4pm Tue–Sun (Thu–Sun in winter)

USS Constitution Museum: open 10am–5pm daily (9am–6pm summer) ▪ Donation

▪ Try some pub grub at the atmospheric 18th-century Warren Tavern (2 Pleasant St).

▪ Visitors must pass through a metal detector to board the *USS Constitution*.

🔟 ⭐ New England Aquarium

The sea pervades nearly every aspect of Boston life, so it's only appropriate that the New England Aquarium is one of the city's most popular attractions. What sets this aquarium apart from many similar institutions is its commitment not only to presenting an exciting environment to learn about marine life, but also to conserving the natural habitats of its thousands of gilled, feathered, and whiskered inhabitants.

① Penguin Pool
Four species of penguins – northern and southern Rockhoppers, Little Blue, and African – coexist happily here, frolicking on the central island **(right)** and taking dips in the pool.

② Yawkey Coral Reef Center
This exhibit reveals a closeup look at species found inhabiting the coral reefs of the Caribbean, including long-spined sea urchins and gently swaying garden eels that burrow together in colonies.

③ Edge of the Sea
For those not content to merely gaze at fish behind glass, the Edge of the Sea tidepool exhibit puts marine life at visitors' fingertips – literally. Inside a ground-level fiberglass tank, the New England seashore is recreated in all its diversity.

④ Harbor Seal Tanks
Harbor seals **(below)** swim, feed, and play in specially designed tanks outside the aquarium. All have either been born in captivity or rescued and deemed unfit for release into the wild.

⑤ Marine Mammal Center
Observe Northern fur seals as they frolic in an open-air exhibit at the edge of the Boston Harbor. Meet the seals and sea lions face-to-face at the large observation deck.

⑥ Tropical Gallery
A Pacific coral reef bustles with unicorn tangs, bird wrasses, and blue-striped cleaner fish, to name but a few of the brightly colored inhabitants **(above)** of these tanks, filled with painted artificial coral. Children will love spotting the Nemo-like clownfish.

9 Whale Watch

The aquarium's whale watch ships (Apr–Oct only) provide an unparalleled glimpse into the life cycles of the world's largest mammals. *Voyager III* steams well outside Boston Harbor to the Stellwagen Bank, a prime feeding area for pods of whales.

7 Giant Ocean Tank

Displaying a spectacular four-story Caribbean reef, the Giant Ocean Tank **(above)** teems with sea turtles, sharks, moray eels, brightly colored tropical fish, and scores of other species in its 200,000-gallon (900,000-liter) space.

10 Amazing Jellies

A 5,000-sq-ft (465-sq-m) nine-tank exhibit shows off thousands of these brainless, boneless, bloodless creatures, including moon jellies and sea nettles.

THE AQUARIUM'S MISSION

The aquarium's aim, first and foremost, is to instigate and support marine conservation. Its Conservation Action Fund has fought on behalf of endangered marine animals worldwide, helping to protect humpback whales in the South Pacific, sea turtles in New England, and dolphins in Peru.

NEED TO KNOW

MAP R3 ■ Central Wharf ■ 617 973 5200 ■ www.neaq.org for general info, including current IMAX features ■ "T" station: Aquarium (blue line)

Open 9am–5pm Mon–Fri, 9am–6pm Sat & Sun (extended hours Jul–Aug)

Adm: adults $26.95; seniors $24.95; children (aged 3–11) $17.95; under 3s free

Whale Watch: 617 973 5206 for reservations and rate information

IMAX: call 866 815 IMAX (4629) for show times; Adm: adults $9.95; seniors and children (aged 3–11) $7.95

■ If the aquarium has not convinced you to remove fish from your diet, visit Legal Harborside for a moderately priced meal *(see p68)*. Quick, quality bites from around the globe can also be had at the Quincy Market food hall, three blocks away.

■ Purchase discount combo tickets for the aquarium along with an IMAX film or a whale-watching excursion.

8 Shark and Ray Touch Tank

One of the largest of its kind in the country, this mangrove-themed tank **(above)** has shallow edges and viewing windows, allowing visitors to roll up their sleeves to feel the velvety wings of stingrays and the abrasive skin of sharks.

Key to Floor Plan
- First floor
- Second floor
- Third floor

The Top 10
of Everything

**Northern Avenue Bridge and
skyscrapers, Boston**

TOP10 Moments in Boston History

Battle of Concord Bridge

1 1630: Boston Founded

Under the leadership of John Winthrop *(see p44)*, English Puritans moved from overcrowded Charlestown and colonized the Shawmut Peninsula. Permission was granted from its sole English inhabitant, Anglican cleric William Blaxton. Their city on the hill was named Boston in honor of the native English town of their leaders.

2 1636: Harvard Created

Boston's Puritan leaders established a college at Newtowne (later Cambridge) to educate future generations of clergy. When young Charlestown minister John Harvard died two years later and left his books and half his money to the college, it was renamed Harvard in his memory *(see p20)*.

Carved detail, Boston Public Library

3 1775: American Revolution

Friction between colonists and the British Crown had been building for more than a decade when British troops marched on Lexington to confiscate rebel weapons. Forewarned by Paul Revere *(see p44)*, local militia, known as the Minute Men, skirmished with British regulars on Lexington Green. During the second confrontation at Concord, "the shot heard round the world" marked the beginning of the Revolution, which ended in American independence with the 1783 Treaty of Paris.

4 1845: Irish Arrived

Irish citizens, fleeing the devastating potato famine in their country, arrived in Boston in tens of thousands, many eventually settling in the south of the city. By 1900, the Irish were the dominant ethnic group in Boston. They flexed their political muscle accordingly, culminating in the election of John F. Kennedy *(see p45)* as president in 1960.

5 1848: Boston Public Library Founded

The Boston Public Library was established as the first publicly supported municipal library in the US. In 1895 the library moved into the Italianate "palace of the people" on Copley Square *(see p87)*.

6 1863: Black Boston Went to War

Following decades of agitation to abolish slavery, the city sent the country's first African-American regiment to join Union forces in the Civil War. The regiment was honored by the Shaw Memorial on Boston Common *(see p18)*.

7 1897: Subway Opened

The Tremont Street subway, the first underground in the US, was opened on September 1 to ease road congestion. It cost $4.4 million to construct and the initial fare was five cents. The Metropolitan Boston Transit Authority (MBTA) now transports 1.2 million people daily.

Zakim Bridge

(8) 1958: Freedom Trail Opened

This historical walking tour connects the city's sights. It was based on a 1951 Boston Herald Traveler column by William Scofield, and was the first of its kind in the US *(see p12)*.

(9) 2007: The Big Dig

The $15 billion highway project to alleviate traffic congestion was completed in 2007, leaving in its place the Rose Kennedy Greenway Park and the soaring Zakim Bridge, the world's widest cable-stayed bridge.

Boston Marathon bombing tributes

(10) 2013: Boston Marathon Bombing

On April 15, 2013, two terrorist bombs exploded near the finish line of the Boston Marathon, killing three people and injuring 264. Following the attack, one perpetrator was killed by the police; the other was convicted and sentenced to death in 2015.

TOP 10 INNOVATIONS

1 Sewing Machine
Elias Howe invented the sewing machine in Cambridge in 1845, but spent decades securing patent rights.

2 Surgical Anesthesia
Ether was first used to anesthetize patients at Massachusetts General Hospital in 1846.

3 Telephone
Alexander Graham Bell invented the telephone in his Boston laboratory in 1876.

Bell's telephone

4 Safety Razor
Bostonian King Camp Gillette invented the safety razor with disposable blades in 1901.

5 Mutual Fund
Massachusetts Investors Trust opened in 1924 as the first modern mutual fund that pooled investors' money to purchase portfolio stocks.

6 Programmable Digital Computer
A Harvard team built the first programmable digital computer, Mark 1, in 1946. Its 750,000 components weighed about 10,000 lb (454 kg).

7 Microwave Oven
A Raytheon company engineer placed popcorn in front of a radar tube in 1946 and discovered the principle behind the microwave oven.

8 Instant Film
Cambridge, Massachusetts, inventor Edwin Land devised the Polaroid camera, launched in 1948.

9 E-mail
Ray Tomlinson, an engineer at Bolt, Beranek, and Newman in Cambridge, sent the first e-mail message in 1971.

10 Facebook
Harvard student Mark Zuckerberg posted the first message to Facemash (social network site Facebook's predecessor) in 2003.

Figures in Boston History

① John Winthrop
(1587–1649)

Acting on a daring plan put together by English Puritans in 1629, John Winthrop led approximately 800 settlers to the New World to build a godly civilization in the wilderness. He settled his Puritan charges at Boston in 1630 (see p42) and served as governor of the Massachusetts Bay Colony until his death.

John Winthrop

② Increase Mather
(1639–1723)

Harvard-educated preacher Increase Mather solidified the hold of Puritan theologians on the Massachusetts government. When William III took the English Crown, Mather persuaded the king to grant a charter that gave the colony the right to elect the council of the governor in 1691. His influence was later undermined by his support of the 1692 Salem witch trials.

Samuel Adams

③ Samuel Adams
(1722–1803)

Failed businessman Samuel Adams became Boston's master politician in the eventful years leading up to the Revolution (see p14). Adams signed the Declaration of Independence and served in both of the Continental Congresses. He later became the governor of Massachusetts, and joined Paul Revere to lay the cornerstone of the State House (see p15) in 1795.

④ Paul Revere
(1735–1818)

Best known for his "midnight ride" to forewarn the rebels of the British march on Concord, Revere served the American Revolution as organizer, messenger, and propagandist. A gifted silversmith with many pieces in the Museum of Fine Arts (see p28–31), he founded the metalworking firm that gilded the State House dome and sheathed the hull of the USS *Constitution*.

⑤ Harrison Gray Otis
(1765–1848)

In the 1790s, Harrison Gray Otis and James Mason transformed Beacon Hill from a hilly pasture into a chic neighborhood that embodies the Federal building style. Otis championed the architecture of Charles Bulfinch, and three of his Bulfinch-designed houses still grace Beacon Hill, including the one now known as Harrison Gray Otis House (see p82).

⑥ Donald McKay
(1810–1880)

McKay built the largest and swiftest of the great clipper ships in his East Boston shipyard in 1850. The speedy vessels revolutionized long-distance shipping at the time of the California gold rush and gave Boston its last glory days as a mercantile port before the rise of rail transportation.

⑦ Mary Baker Eddy
(1821–1910)

After recovering from a major accident, Eddy wrote *Science and Health with Key to the Scriptures*, the basis of Christian Science. She founded a church in Boston in 1879, and in 1892 reorganized it as the First Church of Christ, Scientist *(see p88)*. Eddy also established the Pulitzer prize-winning *Christian Science Monitor* newspaper in 1908.

8 James Michael Curley
(1874–1958)

Self-proclaimed champion of "the little people," Curley used patronage and Irish pride to retain a stranglehold on Boston politics from his election as mayor in 1914 until his defeat at the polls in 1949. Known as "the rascal king" he embodied political corruption but created many enduring public works.

James Michael Curley

9 John F. Kennedy
(1917–1963)

Grandson of Irish-American mayor John "Honey Fitz" Fitzgerald and son of ambassador Joseph Kennedy, John F. Kennedy represented Boston in both houses of the US Congress before he became the first Roman Catholic elected president of the United States. The presidential library at Columbia Point recounts the story of his brief, but intense, period in office *(see p133)*.

10 W. Arthur Garrity, Jr.
(1920–1999)

In 1974, US District Court judge Garrity ruled that African-American students had been denied their constitutional rights to the best available education. His desegregation plan for Boston's 200 schools set off protests, some violent, in predominantly white neighborhoods.

LITERARY BOSTONIANS

Dorothy West

1 Anne Bradstreet
Bradstreet (c.1612–72) was America's first poet, publishing *The Tenth Muse, Lately Sprung Up in America* in 1650.

2 Ralph Waldo Emerson
Poet and philosopher, Emerson (1803–82) espoused transcendentalism as well as pioneering American literary independence.

3 Henry Wadsworth Longfellow
Known for epic poems such as *Hiawatha*, Longfellow (1807–82) also translated Dante.

4 Louisa May Alcott
Little Women sealed the literary fame of Alcott (1832–88), but she also acted as a nurse in the Civil War.

5 Henry James
Master of sonorous prose, James (1843–1916) is considered one of the creators of the psychological novel.

6 Dorothy West
African-American novelist and essayist, West (1907–98) made sharp observations about class and race conflicts.

7 Robert Lowell
The "confessional poetry" of Lowell (1917–77) went on to influence a whole generation of writers.

8 Robert Parker
Scholar of mystery literature, Parker (1932–2010) is best known for his signature detective Spenser.

9 Robert Pinsky
Poet, critic, and translator, Pinsky (b.1940) served as US poet laureate and now teaches at Boston University.

10 Dennis Lehane
Novelist Dennis Lehane (b.1965) brings a dark, tragic vision to the working-class neighborhoods of Boston.

Waterfront Areas

The Esplanade

1 The Esplanade
MAP M3

Provided the Charles River Basin has not frozen over, collegiate rowing crews, canoeists, small sailboats, and the occasional coast guard patrol all share the waters off the Esplanade. Find a bench facing the water and take in the scene.

2 Castle Island Reservation
2010 Day Blvd, South Boston
617 727 5290

Connected to the mainland via an earthen causeway and crowned by the c.1851 Fort Independence, Castle Island is New England's oldest continually fortified site *(see p132)*. Aside from exploring the fort's bunkers and tunnels (in season), visitors enjoy fine panoramic views of Boston Harbor.

3 Constitution Beach
Bennington St, East Boston

Views of Downtown don't get much better than those from this tastefully revitalized beach and park area in East Boston. A clean beach, picnic areas, and lifeguards make this a favorite with families.

4 Long Wharf
MAP R2

The modern Marriott Hotel masks Long Wharf's 300 years of indispensability to Boston's merchant industry. Given the wharf's deep frontage and proximity to waterfront warehouses, the biggest ships of their day could dock here. Today, ferry services and cruise vessels depart from here, creating a spirited dock scene, and there's excellent waterside dining at the restaurant Legal Sea Foods.

5 Fish Pier

By 1926 – 12 years after its construction – the Greco-Roman style Commonwealth Pier (aka Fish Pier) had become the world's busiest and largest fish market. The day's catch is still brought to the early morning market here. Sample some of it in hearty chowders at the legendary No Name Restaurant *(see p69)*.

6 Fort Point Channel
MAP H5

Fort Point has lured artists to the neighborhood with affordable studio space in old warehouse buildings. Open studios in May and October offer a peek inside and a chance to bag a bargain on artwork. Where artists go, gentrification is sure to follow: the neighborhood now boasts the $300-million Federal Courthouse and trendy cafés and restaurants.

Fort Point Channel

⑦ Christopher Columbus Park
MAP P2

Featuring an Italian marble sculpture of the seafaring Genoan, Christopher Columbus Park is among the North End's best-kept secrets. Vine-encrusted arches, manicured gardens, and sweeping harbor and skyline views make this a place to linger.

Rowes Wharf

⑧ Rowes Wharf
MAP R3

Framed by the colossal atrium of the Boston Harbor Hotel *(see p146)*, Rowes Wharf is a popular docking spot for the high-end harbor cruise outfits and is a luxurious contrast to the city's grittier, saltier working docks. The hotel sponsors free concerts and film screenings on summer evenings.

⑨ Puopolo Park
MAP H2

North End's Puopolo Park boasts supreme frontage on the harbor, looking out toward Charlestown. On warm days, the neighborhood's old guard enjoys a game of bocce (bowls). Nearby, kids play baseball or splash around in the outdoor pool.

⑩ Charles River Locks and Dam
MAP F2

This dam controls water levels in the basin below and maintains separation of the river from the harbor. A series of locks permits boats to pass from one body of water to the other.

TOP 10 VIEWS

Weeks Footbridge

1 Prudential Skywalk
Jaw-dropping panoramic views from a 50th-floor observatory (*see p51*).

2 Longfellow Bridge
MAP M2
The entire Charles River Basin becomes your oyster on the "T" between Kendall and Charles/MGH stops.

3 Bunker Hill Monument
Climb to the capstone to see all of Charlestown, Cambridge, and Boston laid out before you (*see p36*).

4 Spirit of Boston Cruises
World Trade Center ▪ 866 310 2469
Ply the harbor waters and admire unrivaled city views as you enjoy brunch, lunch, cocktails, or dinner.

5 Charlestown Bridge
MAP G2
This bridge offers splendid harbor and Downtown vistas.

6 John J. Moakley Courthouse Park
This beautiful waterfront park has fine views of the towering Financial District.

7 Hyatt Regency Cambridge
MAP C4 ▪ 575 Memorial Drive, Cambridge ▪ 617 492 1234
Gaze across the Charles River from the hotel's Zephyr Lounge.

8 Weeks Footbridge
MAP B2
A prime spectator spot during the Head of the Charles Regatta (*see p77*).

9 Dorchester Heights Monument
The park around this commemorative spire offers broad views of the harbor.

10 Hyatt Boston Harbor
101 Harborside Drive, East Boston ▪ 617 568 1234
The Hyatt's Harborside Grill and Patio boasts panoramic Boston views.

🔟 Off the Beaten Path

Sports Museum of New England

① Sports Museum of New England

MAP P1 ■ TD Garden, 100 Legends Way ■ 617 624 1234 ■ Open 10am–4pm Mon–Sat, 11am–4pm Sun; closed on specific event days, see website ■ Adm ■ www.sportsmuseum.org

Spread over two floors above the TD Garden, home of the Bruins (ice hockey) and Celtics (basketball), are displays on all the city's renowned teams, as well as items such as a section of the old wooden seats from the original Boston Garden, where you can sit and watch historic games on a big screen.

② Longfellow House and Washington's Headquarters

In 1775–6, the Federal house served as George Washington's headquarters during the siege of Boston. Over half a century later it was home to legendary American poet Henry Wadsworth Longfellow and his family (see p124).

③ Printing Office of Edes and Gill

MAP Q1 ■ Clough House, 21 Unity St ■ 617 858 8231 ■ Open mid-Apr–May: 11am–5pm Fri–Sun; Jun–Oct: 11am–5:30pm daily ■ www.bostongazette.org

Visitors can interact with costumed historians working at 18th-century printing presses, and learn about the critical role the *Boston Gazette* played in sparking the Revolution.

④ Mapparium

MAP K6 ■ 200 Massachusetts Ave ■ 617 450 7000 ■ Open 10am–4pm Tue–Sun ■ Adm ■ www.marybakereddylibrary.org

The oddly fascinating Mapparium is a stained-glass globe the size of a large room that you view from the inside as you stroll through it along a glass walkway. Illuminated by LED lighting, the countries represented on the globe's surface are those that existed when it was built in 1935. Fabulous acoustics allow whispers to be heard everywhere within the space. The Mapparium is located in the Mary Baker Eddy Library, which also features a small museum dedicated to Eddy and the Christian Science religion she founded (see p44–5).

Mapparium

⑤ The New England Holocaust Memorial

MAP Q4 ■ Between Congress and Union Sts

Six luminous, glass towers soar above a black granite path bordered by lawns and trees. The structures represents the six main death camps, and the six million Jews who died during the six years of World War II.

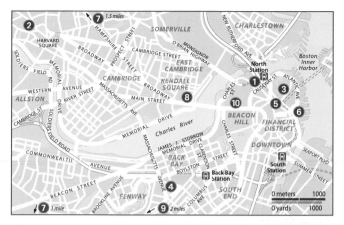

6 Ghosts and Gravestones
MAP R3 ■ 200 Atlantic Ave
■ 866 754 9136 ■ Adm ■ www.
ghostsandgravestones.com
Hop on the black trolley of doom with a gravedigger guide for a "frightseeing" tour of the city's most haunted spots, and visit the site of New England's greatest grave-robbing scandal.

7 Museum of Bad Art
55 Davis Sq, Somerville and
46 Tappan St, Brookline ■ Opening hours vary; see website for details
■ www.museumofbadart.org
MOBA's very special collection of "art too bad to be ignored" is spread over two locations in the city and features works such as *Woman Riding Crustacean* and *Drilling for Eggs*. Each piece is accompanied by an often hilarious commentary.

8 Paddle the Charles River
MAP E3 ■ Charles River Canoe and Kayak, Broad Canal Way, Kendall Square, Cambridge ■ 617 965 5110
■ Adm ■ www.paddleboston.com
What better way to get a whole new perspective on Boston than by seeing it from the water? Visitors can rent their own canoe, kayak, paddleboat, or paddleboard or join a tour and paddle with a group. Options include a Skyline and Sunset Kayak Tour, a Barbecue Picnic Tour, and a guided Eco-Tour.

Samuel Adams Brewery

9 Samuel Adams Brewery
30 Germania St ■ 617 368 5080
■ For tours, visit www.samueladams.com/brewery-and-craft/ourbrewery
The lively tour of the Samuel Adams craft brewery takes you through the process and, yes, offers free tastings of Samuel Adams' famous beers.

10 Paul S. Russell, MD Museum of Medical History and Innovation
MAP N2 ■ Massachusetts General Hospital, 2 North Grove St ■ 617 724 8009 ■ Open 9am–5pm Mon–Fri
■ www.massgeneral.org/museum
This small museum traces medical innovation with engaging interactive displays, artifacts, and expert guides. The nearby Ether Dome was the site of the first successful use of ether as an anesthetic in a public surgery.

🔟 Activities for Children

Children's Museum

a science playground where tracks, balls, and bubbles encourage kids to investigate, and make learning fun.

3 Swan Boats
MAP N4 ■ Public Garden
■ 617 522 1966 ■ Open mid-Apr–mid-Sep: usually 10am–5pm daily ■ Adm
If Boston were to have a mascot, it would likely sport white feathers and a graceful, arching neck. The swan boats have been a Public Garden *(see p19)* fixture since the first fleet glided onto the pond here in 1877.

1 Boston Duck Tours
MAP K6 ■ Prudential Center and Museum of Science
■ 617 267 3825 ■ Open mid-Mar–Nov: 9am–dusk daily ■ Adm
■ www.bostonducktours.com
Board a refurbished, World War II-era amphibious vehicle that plies the Charles River as smoothly as it navigates Back Bay streets. This historic tour encompasses all the peninsula and is conducted by informative, entertaining guides who are great at keeping kids engaged.

Boston Duck Tours

4 Museum of Science
Hands-on learning exhibits, such as assembling animal skeletons or building a computer model, teach children the thrill of discovery. The Omni Theater delights with its fast-paced IMAX projections, while the planetarium places the cosmos within reach. There are also 4-D film presentations and a butterfly garden *(see pp16–17)*.

2 Children's Museum
MAP R5 ■ 300 Congress St
■ 617 426 6500 ■ Open 10am–5pm daily, to 9pm Fri ■ Adm ■ www.bostonchildrensmuseum.org
This venerable funhouse pioneered the interactive-exhibit concept now found in museums worldwide. It includes a climbing wall, a Big Dig-style *(see p43)* construction zone, and

5 New England Aquarium
The aquarium goes to great lengths to keep kids entertained through a variety of interactive displays. Nothing illustrates this better than the Edge of the Sea exhibit, where children can touch some of the region's typical tidepool dwellers *(see pp38–9)*.

Loggerhead sea turtle at the New England Aquarium

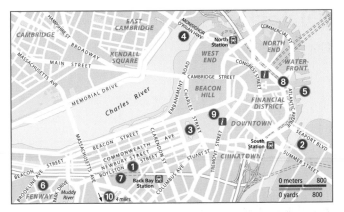

6 Fenway Park

MAP D5 ▪ 4 Yawkey Way
▪ 617 267 1700 ▪ Check www.redsox.
com for schedule

For children with even the slightest interest in sports, a Red Sox game at legendary Fenway Park (see p117) is pure magic. Fans always feel part of the action at the country's most intimate professional baseball park.

7 Prudential Skywalk

MAP K6 ▪ 800 Boylston St
▪ 617 859 0648 ▪ Open Mar–Oct: 10am–10pm daily; Nov–Feb: 10am–8pm daily ▪ Adm

Located on the 50th floor of the Prudential Tower (see p88), this observatory provides a rewarding Boston geography lesson. Should the jaw-dropping, 360-degree views not keep the youngsters enthralled, the audio–video tours of Boston's neighborhoods will. The swift, ear-popping elevator ride to the top is also a thrill.

8 Greenway Carousel

MAP P1 ▪ Rose Kennedy Greenway ▪ www.rosekennedy greenway.org

Set inside the Rose Kennedy Greenway, the linear green parkland in the heart of Boston, this charming carousel features traditionally hand-carved figures of local animals such as a squirrel, turtle, cod, lobster, whale, butterfly, and more. It is also accessible to individuals with disabilities.

Frog statue beside Frog Pond

9 Frog Pond

MAP M4 ▪ Boston Common

As soon as temperatures dip below freezing, kids flock to quaint Frog Pond for ice skating and hot chocolate at the adjacent hut. Boston's oft-oppressive summer days lure them back for splashing and fun beneath the central fountain (see pp18–19).

10 Franklin Park Zoo

1 Franklin Park Rd, Dorchester
▪ 617 541 5466 ▪ Open 10am–5pm Mon–Fri, 10am–6pm Sat–Sun (Oct–Mar: 10am–4pm daily) ▪ Adm
▪ www.zoonewengland.com

Boston's urban zoo, dating back to 1913, houses over 200 species of animals. Its Tropical Forest section houses gorillas, leopards, and other exotic creatures. Bird's World showcases and provides a safe environment for dozens of species. The petting zoo allows kids to get close to animals of the decidedly huggable kind.

TOP 10 **Boston for Free**

USS *Constitution*

1 Charlestown Navy Yard

The Charlestown Navy Yard is home to the USS *Constitution*, the famous Revolutionary War-era frigate known as "Old Ironsides". Also here is the 1943 destroyer USS *Cassin Young*. Both admission and the ranger-led tours of the ships are free *(see pp36–7)*.

2 Hatch Shell

Fridays from June to August are free, family-friendly movie nights at the Hatch Shell, located on the banks of the Charles River. The Hatch Shell also hosts free concerts throughout the year, including Boston Pops' Fourth of July concert *(see p60)*.

3 Mount Auburn Cemetery

580 Mt Auburn St, Cambridge ▪ **617 547 7105** ▪ **www.mountauburn.org**

One of the best places to take a walk in the city is historic Mount Auburn Cemetery, which serves as a park, botanical garden and arboretum, as well as the final resting place of luminaries ranging from poet Henry Wadsworth Longfellow to inventor Buckminster Fuller. The stunningly beautiful 0.3-sq mile- (0.7-sq km-) grounds feature 3 miles (5 km) of walking trails and miles of quiet roadways.

4 Black Heritage Trail

In the 19th century, Boston's thriving black community was a driving force in the fight to end slavery; in the 20th century, to achieve equality. A free National Park Service tour of the Black Heritage Trail *(see p83)* visits a diverse range of historic homes, schools, and businesses that tell the story of Boston's early African-American citizens. Included are visits to the first black public school in America and the 1806 African Meeting House.

5 Freedom Trail

One of the most popular activities for visitors in Boston is walking the self-guided Freedom Trail. Touring the trail is free, as are entering all but three of the 16 sites and attractions along the way. Allow at least half a day for this stroll through history *(see pp12–13)*.

Freedom Trail Town Crier

6 Harvard Square

MAP C2 ▪ **www.harvard square.com**

One of Boston's liveliest public spaces is also a great place for people-watching. There are almost always buskers performing, and it hosts a regular schedule of events including outdoor, free live musical and theater performances. In September, thousands of locals come to take part in the free, one-night RiverSing to celebrate the fall equinox.

Harvard Square

7 Shakespeare on Boston Common

The Commonwealth Shakespeare Company performs one of the Bard's plays free-of-charge on Boston Common each July and August. Perfomances are often preceded by free musical concerts (see p19).

8 Boston HarborWalk
www.bostonharborwalk.com

HarborWalk is actually a collection of waterfront walkways that connect public parks, historic sites, and points of interest from Charlestown to South Boston. An ideal place for cycling, walking, or rollerblading, when completed it will stretch an impressive 47 miles (75 km).

Stretch of Boston HarborWalk

9 Fort Independence

Fort Independence, on Castle Island (see p46) at the entrance to Boston's inner harbor, was a cutting-edge military defense system when it was begun in 1834. Free tours are available in summer. Sullivan's hot-dog stand nearby is legendary.

10 Free Guided Tours

There are many free guided tours available around Boston. Three of the most popular are to the Old State House (see p101), the Boston Public Library (see p87), and the Samual Adams Brewery (see p49). Audissey Guides (www.audisseyguides.com) offer free audio walking tours to the Boston Gardens, Downtown Boston, the HarborWalk, and the Fort Point Channel neighborhood.

MONEY SAVING TIPS

BosTix ticket booth

1 CityPass
A CityPass ($49) gives discounted access to many sights (www.citypass.com).

2 Go Boston Card
Save up to 55 percent on entry to a wide range of sights with this card. Buy online at www.smartdestinations.com

3 Public Transit Passes
A LinkPass allows unlimited travel on subways, buses, and ferries (see p138).

4 Museum Admission
Many Boston museums are free, or offer discounted or pay-what-you-want admission, at certain times.

5 Bargain Tickets
BosTix kiosks sell half-price tickets to many events from 10am on the day of performance (11am Sun).

6 Special Discounts
Student and senior citizen discounts are often available with identification.

7 College Galleries
College and university art galleries offer some of the city's most provocative exhibitions, with free admission.

8 Symphony Savings
Cheap last-minute tickets for some Boston Symphony Orchestra performances are available at Symphony Hall (see p60) on Tue, Thu, and Fri.

9 Theater Deals
The Huntington Theatre (www.huntingtontheatre.org) has $30 tickets for under-35s; the American Repertory Theatre (see p124) usually sells cheap day-of-show tickets for students.

10 Music Schools
Berklee Performance Center (see p61) offers discounted performances. The New England Conservatory holds free performances at Jordan Hall (see p61).

Boston Harbor Islands

1 Deer Island

Accessed by a causeway attaching the island to the mainland, part of the island was opened in 2006 for recreation and walking – with dramatic views of the Boston skyline. Deer Island is also known for its impressive, state-of-the-art $3.8 billion sewage treatment plant. Distinguished by 12 gigantic egg-shaped digesters, it was key to cleaning up Boston Harbor.

Peddocks Island

2 Peddocks Island

Peddocks is one of Boston Harbor's largest and most diverse islands. Hiking trails circle a pond, salt marsh, and coastal forest, and pass by Fort Andrews, which was active in harbor defense from 1904 through to World War II. The island is known for the beach plums and wild roses which bloom profusely in the dunes. A visitor center and campsite make it an overnight destination.

3 Lovells Island

Known for its extensive dunes, Lovells also has an unsupervised swimming beach. Extensive hiking trails lead across the dunes and through woodlands. The remains of Fort Standish, which was active during the Spanish American War and World War I, can also be explored.

4 Grape and Bumpkin Islands

Both these islands are a delight for naturalists – Bumpkin for its wildflowers, raspberries, and bayberries, Grape for its wild roses and bird life. On Bumpkin Island, hiking trails pass the ruins of a farmhouse and 19th-century children's hospital, which also housed German prisoners rescued from Boston Harbor in World War I, and later polio patients, before burning down in 1945.

5 Georges Island

Islands open May–Oct (information booth at Long Wharf) ▪ 617 223 8666 ▪ www.bostonislands.org
As the terminal for the harbor islands ferry and water shuttles to other islands, Georges Island is the gateway to the Boston Harbor Islands National Park Area, which includes 34 islands enclosed within the curve of Boston Harbor. Visitors can hike, swim, explore historic buildings, view birds, and watch the passing ships. But it is also worth spending time here to explore the massive remains of Civil-War-era Fort Warren and check out the snack bar and gift shop.

6 Spectacle Island

Vastly enlarged by fill from the Big Dig *(see p43)*, Spectacle Island has some of the highest peaks of the harbor islands and the best Boston skyline view. The construction of a café and visitor center has made it one of the most popular of all the harbor islands. Visitors can enjoy 5 miles (8 km) of trails and swimming beaches with lifeguards.

Spectacle Island Beach

Little Brewster Island, with its historic lighthouse

7 Little Brewster Island

Island accessible by tour only: mid-Jun–late Sep: Fri–Sun ▪ Call for schedule ▪ Reservations essential: 617 223 8666 ▪ Adm

Boston Light, the first US lighthouse, was constructed here in 1716 and it remains the last staffed offshore lighthouse in the country. Limited tours visit the small museum and lead visitors up the 76 spiral steps and two ladders to reach the top.

8 Gallops Island

Once the site of a popular summer resort, Gallops also served as quarters for Civil War soldiers, including the Massachusetts 54th Regiment (see p18). The island has an extensive sandy beach, a picnic area, hiking paths, and historic ruins of a former quarantine and immigration station. The Massachusetts Department of Conservation and Recreation has closed the island indefinitely for a thorough environmental clean up.

9 Thompson Island

Open Jun–Aug: Sat & Sun ▪ 617 328 3900 ▪ Ferries depart from EDIC Pier on Summer Street ▪ Adm

A learning center since the 1830s, Thompson is the site of an Outward Bound program serving more than 5,000 students annually. The island's diverse geography includes rocky and sandy shores, a large salt marsh, sumac groves, and a hardwood forest. Killdeer, herons, and shorebirds abound.

10 World's End

Operated by Trustees of Reservations: 1 781 740 6665 ▪ Adm for non-members

This 0.4-sq-mile (1-sq-km) peninsula overlooking Hingham Bay is a geological sibling of the harbor islands, with its two glacial drumlins, rocky beaches, ledges, cliffs, and both salt- and freshwater marshes. Frederick Law Olmsted (see p19) laid out the grounds for a homestead development here in the late 19th century. The homes were never built, but carriage paths, formal plantings, and hedgerows remain. World's End is accessed by road by driving through Hingham.

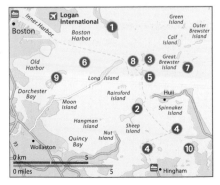

🔟 Day Trips: Historic New England

1 Lexington
Massachusetts ■ **Route 2**
■ **Visitor information: 1875 Massachusetts Ave; 1 781 862 1450** ■ **www.lexingtonchamber.org**

Peaceful Lexington Green marks the first encounter of British soldiers with organized resistance by American revolutionaries. The rebels fortified their courage with a night of drinking at the adjacent Buckman Tavern.

Minuteman statue, Lexington Green

2 Concord
Massachusetts ■ **Route 2**
■ **Visitor information: 58 Main St; 1 978 369 3120** ■ **www.concord chamberofcommerce.org**

Rebels put the Redcoats to rout at North Bridge, Concord's main revolutionary battle site. The town was also the hub of American literature in the mid 19th century, and visitors can tour the homes of Ralph Waldo Emerson, Nathaniel Hawthorne, and Louisa May Alcott. Henry David Thoreau's woodland haunts at Walden Pond now feature hiking trails and a swimming beach.

3 New Bedford
Massachusetts ■ **Routes I-95 & I-195** ■ **Visitor information: 33 William St; 1 508 996 4095** ■ **www.nps.gov/nebe**

During the 19th century, local sailors and whalers plundered the oceans of the world, enriching the port of New Bedford. The National Historic District preserves many fine buildings of the era, and the Whaling Museum gives accounts of the enterprise.

4 Plymouth
Massachusetts ■ **Routes 3 & 44** ■ **Visitor information: 130 Water St; 1 508 747 7525** ■ **www.seeplymouth.com**

The recreated historic village of Plimoth Plantation gives visitors a full immersion into the lives of the first English settlers in Massachusetts. At the harbor, tour the *Mayflower II*. On Thanksgiving, the town celebrates its pilgrim heritage with a parade in period dress.

5 Salem
Massachusetts ■ **Route 1A** ■ **Visitor information: 2 New Liberty St; 1 978 740 1650** ■ **www.nps.gov/sama**

A witch may not have been killed in Salem since 1692, but witchcraft paraphernalia fills many stores, and several sites tell the tale of this dark episode. The city is more proud of its China Trade days (1780s–1880s), which are engagingly recounted on walking tours. Visit the Peabody Essex Museum to see the treasures sea captains brought home.

Salem Witch Museum

Providence, Rhode Island

6 Providence

Rhode Island ▪ Routes 1 or I-95 ▪ Visitor information: 1 Sabin St; 1 401 751 1177 ▪ www.goprovidence.com

Providence is a great walking city: stroll Benefit Street's "mile of history" to see an impressive group of Colonial and Federal houses; or visit Waterplace Park with its pretty walkways along the Providence River. Atwells Avenue on Federal Hill is Providence's Little Italy, bustling with restaurants and cafés.

7 Lowell

Massachusetts ▪ Routes I-93, I-95, & 3 ▪ Visitor information: 246 Market St; 1 978 970 5000 ▪ Adm to Boott Cotton Mills Museum ▪ www. nps.gov/lowe

Lowell was the cradle of the US's Industrial Revolution, where entrepreneurs dug power canals and built America's first textile mills on the Merrimack River. The sites within the National Historical Park tell the parallel stories of a wrenching transformation from an agricultural to industrial lifestyle. A 1920s weave room still thunders away at Boott Cotton Mills Museum.

8 Old Sturbridge Village

Massachusetts ▪ Routes I-90, 20, & 84 ▪ Visitor Center: 380 Main St; 800 733 1830 ▪ www.osv.org

Interpreters in period costume go about their daily lives in a typical 1830s New England village. This large living history museum has more than 40 buildings on 0.3 sq miles (0.8 sq km). Visitors can get a sense of the era by exploring the village common, mill district, and the traditional family farm.

9 Portsmouth

New Hampshire ▪ Routes 1 or I-95 ▪ Visitor information: 500 Market St; 1 603 610 5510 ▪ www. portsmouthchamber.org

Founded in 1623 as Strawbery Banke, the historic houses on Marcy Street document three centuries of city life from earliest settlement through to 20th-century immigration. Picturesque shops, pubs, and restaurants surround Market Square and line the waterfront, and the surrounding leafy streets house fine examples of Federal architecture.

10 Newport

Rhode Island ▪ Routes I-93, 24, & 114 ▪ Visitor information: 23 America's Cup Ave; 1 401 845 9123 ▪ www.gonewport.com

Newport has been a playground for the rich since the late 1860s. Many of the elaborate "cottages" built by 19th-century industrialists are open for tours, including Breakers on Ochre Point Avenue. For natural beauty, hike the 3.6-mile (5.5-km) Cliff Walk overlooking Narragansett Bay and Easton's Beach.

Day Trips: The Beach

① Cape Ann
Routes I-95 & 127 ■ **Visitor information: 33 Commercial St, Gloucester; 1 978 283 1601**

Thirty miles (48 km) north of Boston, the granite brow of Cape Ann juts defiantly into the Atlantic – a rugged landscape of precipitous cliffs and deeply cleft harbors. In Gloucester, a waterfront statue and plaque memorialize the 10,000 local fishermen who have perished at sea since 1623, and the Cape Ann Museum displays maritime paintings. The picturesque harborfront of Rockport is an artists' enclave and is lined with galleries.

Sunset at Gloucester, Cape Ann

② Upper Cape Cod
Routes 3, 6, & 28

The Upper Cape is tranquil and low-key. Watch the boats glide through Cape Cod Canal or take the Shining Sea bikeway from Falmouth village to Woods Hole. If it's beaches you're after, Sandwich's Sandy Neck has huge dunes and excellent bird-watching, but Falmouth's Surf Drive is best for swimmers and Old Silver Beach is tops for sunset views.

③ Mid Cape Cod
Routes 3, 6, & 28

The Mid Cape tends to be congested, especially in the town of Hyannis. But the north shore can be peaceful, with amazing wildlife and stunning views, especially from Gray's Beach in Yarmouth. Warmer water and sandy strands line the south side of Mid Cape, with especially good swimming in Harwich and Dennisport. There's also excellent canoeing and kayaking on the Bass River.

④ Outer Cape Cod
Routes 3 & 6
■ **www.nps.gov/caco**

Here you'll find some of the area's best beaches. The 40-mile (64-km) National Seashore offers great surfing at Coast Guard and Nauset Light, and the beaches of Marconi, Head of the Meadow, and Race Point all have dramatic dunes and great ocean swimming. The artist colonies of Wellfleet and Truro are worth a visit as is Provincetown, a fishing village turned gay resort.

⑤ Nantucket Island
Routes 3 & 6 to Hyannis
■ **Ferry to Nantucket: 1 508 477 8600**
■ **Visitor information: Zero Main St, Nantucket; 1 508 228 1700**
■ **www.nantucketchamber.org**

Nantucket's Whaling Museum tells the tale of the Quaker whalers who made the island prosperous in the 19th century. It now boasts trophy beach houses and million-dollar

Outer Cape Cod

Nantucket Island

yachts. There's kayaking, casting for striped bass from Surfside Beach, or cycling to the village of Sconset with its rose-covered clifftop cottages.

6 Martha's Vineyard
Routes 3 & 28 to Woods Hole
■ **ferry to Vineyard Haven: 1 508 477 8600** ■ **Visitor information: Beach Rd, Vineyard Haven; 1 508 693 0085**
■ **www.mvy.com**

From Vineyard Haven it's a short drive to Oak Bluffs, with its gingerbread cottages and historic carousel. Venture south to Edgartown and the magnificent 19th-century homes of rich whaling captains. Nearby 3-mile (5-km) Katama Beach is a magnet for sun worshipers. On the southwest of the island, Menemsha is a picturesque fishing village and Aquinnah's cliffs offer dramatic hiking.

7 Ipswich
Routes 95, 128, & 133, or 1A
■ **Visitor information: 36 South Main St; 1 978 356 8540** ■ **www.ipswichma.com**

Crane Beach in Ipswich is one of New England's most scenic, with over 4 miles (6.5 km) of white sand, warm water, and outstanding bird-watching. Also on the Crane Estate, you can visit Castle Hill mansion and its lovely Italianate gardens.

8 Newburyport
Routes I-95 & 1 ■ **Visitor information: 38R Merrimac St; 1 978 462 6680**

In the 19th century, Newburyport was a prosperous seaport. The grand three-story mansions along the High Street present a virtual case study in Federal architecture, while boutiques and antiques shops line downtown Merrimac, Water, and State streets. The Parker River National Wildlife Refuge on the adjacent Plum Island is one of the US's top bird-watching sanctuaries, with sandpipers, egrets, and piping plovers among its many residents and visitors.

9 Revere Beach
Routes 1 & 1A ■ **"T" station: Revere Beach/Wonderland**

Established in 1896, Revere Beach was the first public beach in the US. Thanks to a centennial restoration, it's also one of the best, with nearly 3 miles (4.5 km) of clean white sand and clear blue water.

10 Hampton & Rye Beaches
Routes I-95, NH 101, & 1A
■ **Visitor information: 160 Ocean Blvd, Hampton Beach; 1 603 926 8717**
■ **www.hamptonbeach.org**

The New Hampshire coast just south of Portsmouth has extensive sandy beaches. Wallis Sands State Park is ideal for swimming but the best of the rocky overlooks is Rye's Ragged Point picnic area. The social scene, however, is at Hampton Beach. Odiorne Point State Park in Rye has picnic areas and walking trails.

🔟 Performing Arts Venues

Boston Pops Orchestra playing at the Symphony Hall

① Symphony Hall
MAP E6 ■ 301 Massachusetts Ave ■ 617 266 1492 ■ www.bso.org

Opened in 1900, Symphony Hall is one of the world's most acoustically perfect concert venues and is the home of the internationally renowned Boston Symphony Orchestra and the Boston Pops. The BSO commissions new works, hosts world premieres, and frequently welcomes sought-after guest conductors and soloists.

② Citi Performing Arts Center – Wang Theatre
MAP N5 ■ 270 Tremont St ■ 617 482 9393 ■ www.citicenter.org

Capturing the gilded and marbled opulence of its muse, Versailles, the 3,600-seat Wang ranks among the city's most beautiful buildings. The Wang hosts touring productions from Broadway and London's West End as well as dance and opera productions by local companies.

③ Hatch Shell
MAP M3 ■ The Esplanade ■ 617 635 4505

This shell around a performance stage projects music across the Esplanade. Every July 4th (see p76) the Boston Pops Orchestra rings in Independence Day here. Free Friday Flicks (see p52) brings firm family faves such as *The Wizard of Oz* and *Frozen* to the screen, while dance and music events occur almost nightly during summer.

④ Boston Center for the Arts
MAP F5 ■ 539 Tremont St ■ 617 426 5000 ■ www.bcaonline.org

Home to four theater companies, four stages (including Boston's first new theater in 75 years), and a gallery, the BCA is the cornerstone of the South End arts scene. The artists who perform and exhibit here present work as provocative as you might find in New York.

Somerville Theatre

⑤ Somerville Theatre
55 Davis Sq, Somerville ■ 617 625 5700 ■ www.somerville theatreonline.com

Extensive renovation has returned this Davis Square landmark to its original, ornate glory. When it isn't hosting some of the country's finest jazz, world music, and underground rock acts, the Somerville packs audiences in for great-value, second-run movies.

6 New England Conservatory, Jordan Hall
MAP E6 ▪ 30 Gainsborough St ▪ 617 585 1260 ▪ www.necmusic.edu

Dozens of local orchestral and choral ensembles call the NEC's Jordan Hall home. Built at the turn of the 20th century and renowned for its intimacy and impressive acoustics, the New England Conservatory hosts more than 450 free concerts a year.

Berklee Performance Center

7 Boston Opera House
MAP G4 ▪ 539 Washington St ▪ 617 259 3400 ▪ www.bostonoperahouse.com

The Boston Opera House was one of the city's most ornate movie palaces when it opened in 1928. With a $54 million renovation in 2004, the theater was returned to its former glory, and today it presents a steady stream of mostly Broadway shows and is also the home of the Boston Ballet.

8 TD Garden
MAP G2 ▪ 100 Legends Way ▪ 617 624 1050 ▪ www.tdgarden.com

Seating almost 20,000 and with over 3.5 million visitors a year, this arena is home to the NBA's Boston Celtics and the NHL's Boston Bruins, plus the Sports Museum of New England (see p48). It offers a full schedule of concerts, family entertainment, ice shows, public and sporting events.

9 Berklee Performance Center
MAP J6 ▪ 136 Massachusetts Ave ▪ 617 266 7455 ▪ www.berklee.edu/BPC

Berklee, the world's largest independent music college, boasts this premier venue. The great acoustics ensure that some of the most highly distinguished jazz, folk, and world musicians play here.

10 Sanders Theatre
MAP B1 ▪ 45 Quincy St, Cambridge ▪ 617 496 2222

Located in Harvard's splendid Memorial Hall (see p23), this theater has hosted many luminaries over its 120-plus years. Great performers of the past century have graced its intimate stage, including mime artist Marcel Marceau; and Longfellow, Oliver Wendell Holmes, and Ralph Wardo Emerson were among its early audiences.

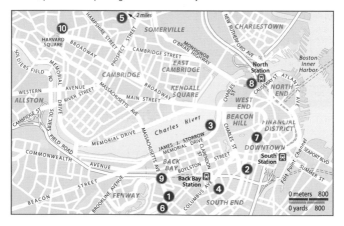

🔟 Dance and Live Music Venues

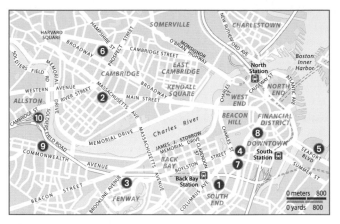

1 The Beehive
MAP M6 ▪ 541 Tremont St
▪ 617 423 0096

The nightly music mix here might sometimes veer toward cabaret or even burlesque, but local jazz musicians are the mainstay for a usually well-dressed, mature crowd at least a decade past their school-days. A convivial bar scene and excellent comfort food round out the appeal of this great night out.

2 The Middle East
The region's alternative rock scene can trace its genesis to this Central Square landmark. This influential venue has launched many careers. Seminal local bands like the Pixies, Mighty Mighty Bosstones, and Morphine all played on The Middle East's three stages. Today, the club continues the tradition, genuinely embracing musicians operating just under the mainstream, popular radar *(see p128)*.

3 House of Blues
MAP D5 ▪ 15 Lansdowne St
▪ 888 693 2583 ▪ Adm

The House of Blues chain was born across the river in Cambridge, and this 2,400-capacity room behind Fenway Park continues the commit-

ment to American music: blues, gospel, jazz, rhythm and blues, and roots-based rock 'n' roll. A Gospel brunch is offered on Sundays, and the restaurant also opens during Red Sox evening home games.

House of Blues

4 Whisky Saigon
The sumptuous, dark interior, glam lighting, and extensive range of designer vodkas combine a stylish high-tech approach with enchanting, old-fashioned romanticism. It is easy

Lauryn Hill performing at Royale

to see why this attention-seekers' paradise has topped various polls, including sexiest bar and best pick-up spot *(see p111)*.

5 Whiskey Priest
MAP H4 ■ 150 Northern Ave
■ 617 426 8111

An Irish gastropub in a prime water-front spot in the Fort Point district, Whiskey Priest has live acoustic music every Wednesday, karaoke on Thursday, DJs on Friday, and live rock bands on Saturday. An impressive menu of over 100 whiskeys is complemented by a wide range of beers. The venue is convenient for the World Trade Center.

6 Ryles
MAP D2 ■ 212 Hampshire St, Cambridge ■ 617 876 9330 ■ Closed Mon ■ Adm

Ryles is one of Inman Square's greatest assets, where jazz musicians come to play and perform. Call ahead to learn if samba or swing lessons are scheduled, and don't miss the good-value Sunday jazz brunch: no cover charge, live jazz, boisterous crowds, and hearty entrées that rarely venture above $10.

7 Royale
Housed in an ornate, bi-level theater, the Royale can accommodate more nightlife denizens than any other Boston club. Top 40, 1980s, Latin, and house music are pumped through the powerful sound system,

while a mixed crowd lounges around on cushy banquettes or throngs the mammoth dance floor *(see p111)*.

8 Orpheum Theatre
MAP G4 ■ 1 Hamilton Pl
■ 617 482 0106 ■ Adm

Boston's oldest music venue, the Orpheum dates from 1852. After serving as a vaudeville house and a movie theater, it has now become a beloved venue for touring rock bands and comedy concerts.

9 Paradise Rock Club
MAP C5 ■ 967 Commonwealth Ave ■ 617 562 8800 ■ Adm

Although no longer in its original Downtown location, the Paradise is the oldest name in Boston rock venues. Icons from the 1970s and 1980s such as Van Halen, the Police, and Blondie first put the club on the map. Today, the Paradise remains true to its rock 'n' roll roots, welcoming nationally recognized acts that favor volume levels north of ten.

Scullers Jazz Club

10 Scullers Jazz Club
MAP C4 ■ 400 Soldiers Field Rd ■ 617 562 4111 ■ Closed Sun ■ Adm

Enthusiastic champion of Latin jazz and emerging artists (for example, Norah Jones and Diana Krall started here), Scullers is also a well-known venue for internationally established musicians. It's a great place to enjoy a drink and an evening of smooth jazz by some of the best performers in the business.

🔟 Gay and Lesbian Hangouts

Classy interior of Club Café

1 Club Café
MAP M6 ■ 209 Columbus Ave

A video lounge and a popular Sunday brunch infallibly bring out the beautiful boys at this multifunctional South End meeting spot with great bar staff. Choose from the casually elegant restaurant, which puts inspired twists on classic continental fare, the mirrored bar area – perfect for scoping the room – and the sleek cocktail lounge out the back.

2 Midway Café
3496 Washington St, Jamaica Plain ■ Adm

Having offered its stage to rockabilly, punk, swing, reggae, and hip-hop acts since 1987, the Midway Café is partially responsible for Jamaica Plain's *(see p133)* youth-driven renaissance. Most nights bring an eclectic, edgy mix of music lovers, both gay and straight. The club's Thursday Women's Dance Night is the most popular lesbian club night in town.

3 dBar
1236 Dorchester Ave ■ 617 265 4490

This popular Dorchester spot has a split personality: trendy neighborhood bistro by day, popular gay dance club at night. "Show Tunes Tuesdays" are a wildly popular sing-along that can get a bit rowdy late in the evening.

The decor features lots of warm wood and brass that creates an inviting atmosphere.

4 Diesel Café
257 Elm St, Somerville

This hipster-filled coffee shop, in the heart of Somerville's bustling Davis Square, is a favorite hangout among the area's young gay and lesbian couples. The varied menu runs the gamut from gourmet coffee drinks and inventive tea concoctions to tasty snacks. Its spacious, relaxed vibe is great for chatting an afternoon away or for making new friends.

5 Machine
MAP E5 ■ 1254 Boylston St ■ Adm

A recent facelift saw Machine absorb the dated, hardcore Ramrod that used to be in the same building. Machine is now a two-story, mostly gay nightclub, that also attracts a growing straight audience with themed nights, including drag shows, karaoke, and a busy dance floor packed, particularly on weekends, with mostly young, beautiful bodies. Male go-go dancers and DJ-led dance nights featuring the best dance music of the 1980s, 1990s, and 2000s help round out the offerings.

Popular nightclub Machine

6 Guerilla Queer Bar
www.thewelcomingcommittee. com/boston#boston-takeovers

This is not a place, but a viral event. On the third Saturday of each month scores, and sometimes hundreds, of gays and lesbians descend on an otherwise vanilla-straight bar or nightclub. The result is fun and uplifting for gays and straights alike –

so much so that it is becoming a nationwide phenomenon. Check the website for the forthcoming venue.

7 The Alley Bar
MAP P3 ■ 275 Washington St ■ 617 263 1449

The Alley has a mellow, sociable vibe, with activities including karaoke, pool tournaments, underwear parties, and other theme nights for men who want to meet men. A big Alley attraction is the Saturday-night Bear Party for full-framed guys and those who love them. There is an upstairs/downstairs set-up which separates the various theme-night crowds from local drinkers.

8 Paradise Bar
MAP D3 ■ 180 Massachusetts Ave, Cambridge ■ 617 868 3000

This Kendall Square club is best known for having live performances by male dancers six nights a week, and for fielding new amateur talent. The upstairs bar shows big-screen movies and concert videos, while downstairs is a dance hall – no high heels allowed.

9 Jacque's Cabaret
One of the oldest names on the Boston gay club scene, Jacque's has been welcoming queer rock bands, drag queens, and their adoring fans for many decades. Garage rock and beer fuel the crowded area around

Jacque's Cabaret

the popular pool tables. Discreetly tucked away behind the Theater District, Jacque's is a lively option every night of the week *(see p111)*.

10 Boston Eagle
MAP F6 ■ 520 Tremont St

A doorway-mounted wooden eagle has welcomed gay men to this sub-terranean South End bar for years. Having no qualms about simply being a gay bar, the Eagle is not a place to dance. The dimly lit bar area is roomy and comfortable; in the back, a mirrored wall captures pool sharks and pinball wizards at work.

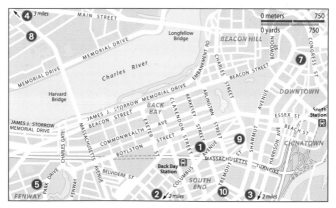

🔟 Restaurants

1 L'Espalier

Adjoining the luxury Mandarin Oriental Hotel *(see p146)*, this is one of Boston's top restaurants, in the heart of fashionable Back Bay. The award-winning, modern French cuisine emphasizes local ingredients, producing dishes such as butter-poached Maine lobster and cocoa-rubbed venison. Only expensive fixed-price and tasting menus are offered during dinner service *(see p93)*.

Elegant L'Espalier

2 Rialto

MAP B2 ▪ Charles Hotel, 1 Bennett St, Cambridge ▪ 617 661 5050 ▪ D only ▪ $$$

Chef Jody Adams takes a luscious and delicately innovative approach to regional Italian cuisine. A green olive and balsamic vinegar sauce perfectly balances the unctuousness of her signature roasted marinated duck. The comfortable and soothing dining room is perfect for special occasions.

Rialto's roast duck

3 Mamma Maria

MAP H3 ▪ 3 North Square ▪ 617 523 0077 ▪ D only ▪ $$

This up-scale eatery is located in a 19th-century row house and is loaded with old-world charm. Its daily changing menu specializes in classic Italian comfort cuisine with just a bit of a twist. For example, the clam pasta features not only famous Falmouth (Cape Cod) clams, but also toasted pine nuts, prosciutto, and sautéed green pea tendrils. Save room for a dessert, such as Nonna's chocolate torte with espresso gelato.

4 Café ArtScience

MAP E3 ▪ 650 Kendall St, Cambridge ▪ 857 999 2193 ▪ $$$

Patrick Kempbell, one of the country's rising chefs, serves an ingredient-driven menu featuring innovative dishes made from local produce. Try the roasted pumpkin soup with goat's cheese and *huitlacoche* (corn fungus) fritter. The restaurant indulges in some nifty science tricks, including drinks that have to be inhaled.

5 Trade

MAP H4 ▪ 540 Atlantic Ave ▪ 617 451 1234 ▪ $$

Trade is the fine-dining anchor to the Greenway Park that links Downtown and the waterfront. Set in the Atlantic Wharf building, it makes use of Mediterranean flavors while remaining true to its New England roots. Both ends of that historic trade route shine in dishes such as braised short rib with Jerusalem artichoke, olives and orange. The light lunches are good value.

6 Toro

MAP F6 ▪ 1704 Washington St ▪ 617 536 4300 ▪ $$$

Chef-owners Ken Oringer and Jamie Bissonnette team up for one of the city's hardest-to-get-into restaurants. The South End hot spot serves a mix of modern and traditional tapas and upscale Latin fare in stylish environs, from a menu filled with trendy imported items and original dishes *(see p111)*.

Menton's exquisite cuisine

7 Menton
MAP H5 ■ 354 Congress St
■ 617 737 0099 ■ D only ■ $$$

Superchef Barbara Lynch's elegant Fort Point dining room regularly receives national-level rave reviews. Diners can choose from one of two tasting menus, with offerings such as lobster and chamomile with fava, hazelnut, and Meyer lemon, or tart of foie gras enhanced with wild ramps, beetroot, and spring onion. All diners at a table are requested to choose the same menu.

8 Craigie On Main
MAP D3 ■ 853 Main St, Cambridge ■ 617 497 5511 ■ $$$

Award-winning chef Tony Maws, acclaimed for his French-inspired nose-to-tail approach to fine dining, presides over a bustling open kitchen facing the dining area, filled with an eclectic mix of diners. The menu changes daily, based on the locally sourced organic ingredients of the day. Head to the bar for its wildly popular gourmet burger.

9 Meritage
MAP H4 ■ 70 Rowes Wharf ■ 617 439 3995
■ $$$

Chef Daniel Bruce showcases perfect pairings of food and wine at this elegant eatery in the Boston Harbor Hotel. Diners choose dishes from either a red/rosé wine menu or a white/sparkling wine menu, as part of his innovative vineyard-to-table philosophy.

10 Harvest
MAP B1 ■ 44 Brattle St, Cambridge ■ 617 868 2255 ■ $$$

Since the 1970s, this relaxed restaurant has been a leader in setting the direction of American cuisine. Chef Mary Dumont reinterprets New England classics, matching monkfish with artichokes and cockles, or filling ricotta gnocchi with butternut squash and sautéing them in pumpkin seed oil.

Bar at Harvest

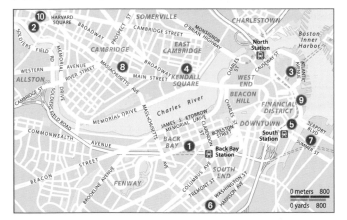

For a key to restaurant price ranges see p85

TOP 10 Spots for Seafood

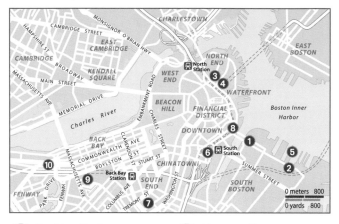

1 Barking Crab
MAP H4 ▪ 88 Sleeper St ▪ 617 426 2722 ▪ $

This colorful fish shack is most congenial in the summer, when diners sit outdoors at picnic tables, but there's also indoor seating with a cozy wood-burner for chillier days. Most of the local fish – cod, haddock, tuna, halibut, clams, and crab – are so fresh that they need only the most simple preparation.

2 Legal Harborside
MAP H3 ▪ Liberty Wharf & other locations ▪ 617 477 2900 ▪ $$

The Seaport flagship of the Legal Sea Foods chain makes dockside dining chic. You'll find a no-frills, casual dining room, oyster bar, and a traditional fish market on level one; there's fine dining featuring beautifully prepared fish on level two; while level three offers a four-season rooftop lounge and bar, with retractable glass roof and walls, serving ocean-fresh sushi and cocktails. All three spaces come with a stunning harbor view.

Legal Harborside

3 Neptune Oyster
MAP H3 ▪ 63 Salem St ▪ 617 742 3474 ▪ $$

Exceptionally fresh choices from the raw bar vie for attention with dishes from the expertly prepared dinner menu. Choose an old favorite, such as clam chowder, or a more daring dish like Spanish octopus with hazelnut romesco. The simple, unfussy dining room ensures that the food is the focus of attention. Reservations are not accepted so arrive early and be prepared to wait in line for a table – it's worth it.

4 Mare Oyster Bar
MAP H3 ▪ 3 Mechanic St ▪ 617 723 4273 ▪ Closed L Mon ▪ $$$

Mare specializes in Italian coastal cuisine. Begin with the raw bar or a trio of crudos, then savor a classic seafood pasta dish or grilled fish – or indulge yourself with a decadent lobster roll on brioche. A few meat dishes are also available. To accompany your meal, enjoy a cocktail or glass of wine from their enticing drinks menu.

5 No Name Restaurant

15½ Fish Pier ▪ 617 423 2705
▪ $

Fish Pier's only restaurant has an intimate relationship with the fishermen who both sell their catch to, and eat at, this bare-bones place. The very basic menu consists mostly of fried fish, while the great chowder is full of what fishermen call "trim" – chunks of whatever has been caught, boned and trimmed that day.

6 O Ya

MAP H5 ▪ 9 East St ▪ 617 654 9900 ▪ Closed L Sun, Mon ▪ $$$

Combining Japanese tradition and American invention, this elegant restaurant proves that good things come in small packages. Half the menu is sushi and sashimi, the other half meat and vegetarian. With six chefs at work, each bite-sized portion is exquisitely executed. Ask for the omakase (tasting) menu and let head chef Tim Cushman wow you with a culinary *tour de force*.

B&G Oysters

7 B&G Oysters

MAP F6 ▪ 550 Tremont St ▪ 617 423 0550 ▪ $$$

This brightly lit underground seafood spot is both oyster bar – there are a dozen varieties ready to be shucked at any moment – and seafood bistro.

8 James Hook & Co.

MAP H5 ▪ 15 Northern Ave ▪ 617 423 5500 ▪ Closed evenings ▪ $

A family-owned business located right on Fort Point Channel, Hook is primarily a broker that supplies

James Hook & Co.

lobster to restaurants throughout the US. However, they also cook lobster, clams, crab, and some fin fish on the spot. Take your order, sit on the sea wall, and chow down. Considered by many the best place to eat in Boston.

9 Summer Shack

MAP K6 ▪ 50 Dalton St ▪ 617 867 9955 ▪ Closed L Mon–Fri Nov–Mar ▪ $$

Boston celebrity chef Jasper White literally wrote the book on lobster, but he's just as adept with wood-grilled fresh fish and delicate fried shellfish. A fabulous raw bar and colorful summer fish-shack atmosphere match well with the extensive beer list. It's a great place to bring kids who like to crack their own crabs.

10 Island Creek Oyster Bar

MAP D5 ▪ 500 Commonwealth Ave ▪ 617 532 5300 ▪ Closed L Mon–Sat ▪ $$$

Partly owned by the Duxbury oyster farm of the same name, this upscale yet casual restaurant excels at shellfish (including eight varieties of New England oysters) and does great things with fin fish, too. Their seafood casserole brings together shrimp, lobster, clams, scallops, and cod in a single delectable bowl.

Lobster at Island Creek Oyster Bar

For a key to restaurant price ranges see p85

🔟 Cafés

Comfortable split-level interior of Thinking Cup

1 Thinking Cup
MAP G4 ▪ 165 Tremont St

A cozy place to socialize on Boston Common, Thinking Cup serves teas and Stumptown Coffee. Knowledge-able baristas offer assistance with your choice of espresso drinks or pour-overs. The menu also includes tempting pastries and sandwiches.

2 Wired Puppy
MAP K5 ▪ 250 Newbury St

This coffee shop in the middle of Newbury Street is popular with the local office crowd. Try their artisan espresso, gourmet coffee drinks, and fresh pastries. There's also free use of their computer and Wi-Fi.

3 Caffè Vittoria
MAP Q1 ▪ 296 Hanover St

The jukebox at the largest of North End's Italian cafés is heavily loaded with songs recorded by Frank Sinatra, Tony Bennett, and Al Martino. The menu is long on short coffees and short drinks, including at least seven varieties of grappa, as well as a fair selection of Italian ices.

4 Mike's Pastry
MAP H2 ▪ 300 Hanover St

Mike's is legendary for its 20 or so flavors of fresh cannolis. There is a café where all the baked goodies are available – cupcakes, biscotti, brownies, cakes, pies, cookies, and specialty items – along with gourmet brews. The lines can be long, especially on weekends, but they move quickly.

5 Sonsie
MAP J6 ▪ 327 Newbury St

Although continental breakfast is served, Sonsie doesn't really get going until lunchtime. By dusk, it is full of folks who just stopped in for a post-work drink and ended up making an evening of it. The food – pizza, pasta, and fusion-tinged entrées – deserves more attention than most café-goers give it.

6 Barrington Coffee Roasting Company Café
MAP H5 ▪ 346 Congress St, Fort Point

This western Massachusetts coffee roaster brought its acclaimed selection of single-origin coffees to this artistic neighborhood at Fort Point Channel. There is a second outlet now at Newbury Street. Espresso and drip coffee get equal billing, as many of the lighter roasts are best brewed one drip cup at a time. Regular tasting events are a popular feature.

7 1369 Coffee House

The 1369 Coffee House is as community-based as Starbucks is corporate. It has a definite neighborly atmosphere. The original Inman Square branch has a more interesting cross section of ages and ethnicities but Central Square has sidewalk seating. Both branches serve mostly caffeine drinks and sweets – with sandwiches at lunch (see p127).

8 Dado Tea
MAP C2 ■ 955 Massachusetts Ave, Cambridge ■ MAP B1 ■ 50 Church St, Cambridge

However you like your tea – white, black, or green – this shop has a choice of blends to relish in themselves or as accompaniment to healthy sandwiches, wraps, and salads. Coffee-lovers are also accommodated, but tea rules here.

9 Parish Café
MAP M5 ■ 361 Boylston St

The tables outside Parish Café offer a terrific view of the lower Back Bay street scene. Parish has some of the most creative and delicious sandwiches in the city – designed by chefs of Boston's top restaurants. Comfort-food dishes are also great.

10 Max Brenner
MAP E4 ■ 745 Boylston St

Chocoholics will demand a trip to this celebration of all things cocoa. Savor the Illegal Chocolate Chocolate Chocolate Pancakes, made with 70 percent dark chocolate cream, milk chocolate shavings, spiced pecans and caramelized bananas, or a chocolate martini. There are non-chocolate dishes too, such as smoked mozzarella and mushroom mac 'n' cheese.

Max Brenner's chocolate café

TOP 10 SPOTS TO BREAK YOUR DIET

L. A. Burdick Chocolatiers

1 Finale
MAP M5 ■ 1 Columbus Ave
Try the molten chocolate gateau or rich crème brûlée.

2 L. A. Burdick Chocolatiers
MAP B1 ■ 52D Brattle St, Cambridge
Sinful bonbons and unquestionably Boston's best hot chocolate.

3 Union Square Donuts
20 Bow St, Somerville
Small batches of donuts in sweet and savory flavors.

4 ChocoLee Chocolates
MAP F6 ■ 23 Dartmouth St
Truffles and bonbons by Lee Napoli.

5 Flour Bakery & Café
MAP F6 ■ 1595 Washington St;
MAP R5 ■ 12 Farnsworth St
Delicious cakes, cookies, and cups of excellent coffee.

6 Sugar Heaven
MAP L5 ■ 669 Boylston St
"Penny candy" by the pound for childhood memories.

7 Eldo Cake House
MAP P4 ■ 36 Harrison Ave
Western-style iced cakes and Chinese treats.

8 Lizzy's Ice Cream
MAP B1 ■ 29 Church St, Cambridge
Chopped candy bars and sundae toppings in super-rich ice cream.

9 Langham Boston Chocolate Dessert Buffet
MAP Q4 ■ 250 Franklin St
■ Open Sep–Jun: Sat
A delicious range of French chocolate pastry and sweets.

10 Christina's Homemade Ice Cream
MAP D2 ■ 1255 Cambridge St, Cambridge
Exotic spices and flavors add punch.

Bars

1 Drink
MAP R5 ■ 348 Congress St
■ 617 695 1806

This trendy subterranean bar in the Fort Point district wins praise for its impressive lineup of classic and classically inspired cocktails. Knowledgeable bartenders may quiz you to create a drink to suit your character. The house signature drink here is the Fort Point variation on a Manhattan.

2 Oak Long Bar & Kitchen
MAP L6 ■ 138 St James Ave

The Copley Plaza hotel bar serves a full roster of craft cocktails and a farm-to-table seasonal dining menu. In summer, drinks and meals can be enjoyed on the outdoor patio, which appropriately overlooks the twice-weekly farmers' market.

3 Firebrand Saints
MAP E3 ■ 1 Broadway, Cambridge

The neighborhood bar for MIT students and about half the dot-coms on the East Coast, Firebrand Saints is wildly original, right down to its light-projection streetscapes. Bar food ranging from porchetta sandwiches to poached lobster accompanies the quirky alchemist cocktails.

4 Delux Café
The kind of place that is so special, you want to keep it a secret. The South End's intimate Delux Café attracts a refreshing mix of professionals, bike messengers, and gay boys and girls, all suckers for the bar's kitschy Elvis motif, extensive on-tap beers, and constant broadcast of the Cartoon Network (see p111).

5 Towne Stove & Spirits
MAP E5 ■ 900 Boylston St

While Towne wins rave reviews for its upscale comfort food, the drinks menu may be even better. An eclectic range of cocktails includes the likes of Back-Bacon Manhattan (bourbon, bitters, and bacon-infused vermouth). Less daring guests will also find plenty of classic cocktails to tingle their tastebuds.

6 Les Zygomates
The dinner crowd at Les Zygomates (the French term for the facial muscles that make you smile) is lured by reasonably priced French bistro fare. After 9pm, the sleek, whimsically designed bar area comes alive with young professionals intent on flexing their smile muscles and appreciating the nightly live jazz performances (see p113).

Plush interior of Oak Long Bar & Kitchen

Jazz musicians at Regattabar

7 Regattabar

The giants of jazz often stop at this nautical-themed lounge in Cambridge's Charles Hotel. Drinks may not be extraordinary but the talent is; past visitors have included McCoy Tyner, Ron Carter, and local favorite the Charlie Kolhase Quintet. Shows sell out quickly (see p128).

8 Hawthorne

MAP D5 ■ 500 Commonwealth Ave

This suave craft cocktail bar anchors the nightlife scene at the Hotel Commonwealth in Kenmore Square. Lounge-like in the front, cozy in the back, it's the place to drink and socialize. Creative house cocktails, and the first-rate wine list includes several sparkling wines by the glass.

9 Noir

MAP B1 ■ 1 Bennet St, Cambridge ■ 617 661 8010

In the Charles Hotel, sophisticated bar food complements the equally sophisticated variants on a classic martini. The all-black decor with high-backed banquettes creates a perfect atmosphere for private carrying-on. Waitresses carry flashlights to help you read the menu.

10 Alibi

MAP F3 ■ 215 Charles St

Set in the former drunk tank of the Charles Street Jail (now the posh Liberty Hotel), Alibi retains the bluestone floors and vestiges of the cell walls to form little nooks to lounge in while enjoying a drink or two. The outdoor patio is great for cocktails at sunset.

TOP 10 LOCALLY BREWED BEERS

1 Chamberlain Pale Ale
An English-style pale ale with the delicious, malty middle of its forebears.

2 Harpoon IPA
Ranked among the top domestic and imported India pale ales by *Beer Connoiseur Magazine*.

3 John Harvard's Nut Brown
Try this malty, light ale served at John Harvard's Brew House (33 Dunster St, Cambridge).

4 Samuel Adams Octoberfest
Sam's finest – available only during the autumn – with deep amber coloring and a warm, spicy smoothness.

5 Boston Beer Works Fenway Pale Ale
Don your Red Sox cap and sip a light Fenway Pale at Boston Beer Works (see p120).

6 Samuel Adams Boston Lager
The beer that put Sam back on the brewing map after a 200-year hiatus.

7 Pretty Things Jack D'or
This popular brewer's signature beer is the flavorful "Saison Americain" farmhouse-style ale.

8 Samuel Adams Cherry Wheat Ale
Like a hybrid between champagne and cherry soda; available at most liquor stores.

9 Harpoon UFO Hefeweizen
Unfiltered, Belgian-style brew, with fruity undertones.

10 Clown Shoes Hoppy Feet
Grapefruit and pine on the nose, with dark chocolate and nuts on the palate.

Samuel Adams Octoberfest mugs

Essential Shopping Experiences

Newbury Street

1 Newbury Street

Try as it might, Back Bay's most famous street cannot escape its regional reputation as the city's Beverly Hills' Rodeo Drive. True, both offer stupendous people-watching, sophisticated shopping, chic dining, and prestigious galleries. Yet, with its 19th-century charm and convenient subway stops, Newbury Street out-classes its built-yesterday Left Coast counterpart by far *(see pp24–5)*.

2 Garment District
MAP D2 ■ 200 Broadway, Cambridge

The vintage clothing and bargain-priced trends of the Garment District are every Boston hipster's retort to fashion. Fancy-dress costumes are found on the first floor, but the best deal happens every morning when the shop snips open a vast bale of clothes to sell by the pound.

3 Artists' Open Studios
www.cityofboston.com

Boston's visual artists open their studios to the public on selected spring and fall weekends. Boston's numerous studio events are mostly in converted former warehouses. One of the most popular is the South End Open Studio event. Start at the Boston Center for the Arts *(see p60)*, where there are many studios nearby, and pick up a map for the rest.

4 Copley Place
MAP L6 ■ 100 Huntington Ave

This was among the country's first upscale urban shopping malls. It counts such high-end tenants as Louis Vuitton, Tiffany, Neiman Marcus, and Coach. Footwear addicts are fond of Stuart Weitzman and Jimmy Choo boutiques.

5 Red Sox Team Store
MAP D5 ■ 19 Yawkey Way

With World Series titles dating back to 1903 and the oldest ballpark in professional baseball, the Boston Red Sox engender a fan loyalty matched by few other teams. This memorabilia shop, across the street from Fenway Park *(see p117)*, sells every permutation of hat, jersey, and T-shirt imaginable, as well as signed bats, balls, and gloves, and baseball cards for hardcore collectors.

Red Sox merchandise

6 The Haymarket
MAP Q2 ■ Times are flexible, but roughly dawn–dusk Fri & Sat

This 350-year-old outdoor produce market (note that it is not a farmers' market) still holds undeniable charm for visitors. Witness the feeding frenzy as fishmongers try to under-cut each other on the day's catch, fresh from the piers.

7 Harvard Square Bookstores
MAP B1

Harvard Square's bookstores are some of the most distinguished in the country. The Harvard Coop carries 170,000-plus titles, while Schoenhof's Foreign Books specializes in non-English books. The Harvard Book Store (1256 Massachusetts Ave) stocks countless new and used titles. And the irrepressible Revolution Books (see p126) keeps the red flag flying here with socialist and communist literature.

Charles Street store

Harvard Book Store

8 Charles Street
MAP M3

Charm abounds on this bluest-of-blue-blooded street, studded with antique dealers (see p84), specialty grocers, and modern houseware boutiques. Come nightfall, wrought-iron gas lamps illuminate the brick sidewalks, residents hurry home with wine and fresh flowers, and sleek bistros buzz with excitement.

9 Faneuil Hall Marketplace

With its millions of visitors each year, Faneuil Hall Marketplace would not be found on any best-kept secret list. However, with its central location, rich colonial history, and plethora of food stalls, it offers a unique retail experience. Shoppers can choose from name-brand stores such as Victoria's Secret or the more unusual offerings from New England artisans (see p101).

10 SoWa Open Market
MAP G6 ▪ Ink Block, Harrison Ave

Expect clothing, jewelry, and art at Boston's art and indie design market, held every Sunday in the South End. A farmers' market augments the summer scene as top Boston food trucks feed hungry shoppers.

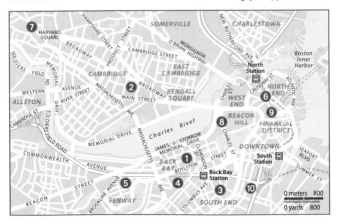

⏹ Festivals and Events

Boston Pops' Fourth of July concert at Hatch Shell on the Esplanade

1 Fourth of July

Given Boston's crucial role in securing independence for the original 13 colonies, Independence Day adopts a certain important here. With parties, barbecues and a fireworks display on the Charles River banks, Boston throws the nation a spectular birthday party.

2 Chinese New Year

Chinatown (see pp106–113) buzzes with the pageantry of the Chinese New Year (held in either January or February). Streets are transformed into patchworks of color, while sidewalk vendors peddle steamed buns, soups, and other Chinese delights. Don't miss the annual parade, held the Saturday following the Lunar New Year.

3 Boston Flower and Garden Show

For a week in March, over 150,000 visitors descend on this indoor exhibition, hosted at various venues, to forget their winter blues and enjoy the spectacular display of bright blooms and fragrant aromas.

4 First Night

Despite the possibility of staggeringly cold weather, the New Year's Eve festivities remain among the most highly anticipated events of Boston's year. A pass grants access to concerts, performances, and museum exhibits throughout the city at a reasonable price, not to mention a dazzling midnight fireworks display over Boston Harbor.

5 Cambridge River Festival

For one day in mid-June the banks of the Charles River in Cambridge host a celebration of the city's lively and diverse population. Musicians and dancers perform and artists sell their wares. Food vendors offer a taste of home.

6 Feast of St. Anthony

The Feast of St. Anthony caps an entire summer of feast holidays in the North End (see pp94–9). On the last weekend in August, from morning well into the night, Hanover Street bulges with revelers, parades, and food vendors giving a vibrant display of the area's old-world Italian spirit.

Feast of St. Anthony

7 Boston Calling

National headliners and new, up-and-coming acts perform live, with non-stop music for three days in May and September at City Hall

Plaza, to sell-out crowds. It's a family-friendly festival, with two stages and a good variety of high-energy performers and musical styles. In recent years, Boston Calling has featured the likes of Beck, the Pixies, Kendrick Lamar, Lorde, and the Alabama Shakes.

8 St. Patrick's Day

Boston's immense Irish-American population explains why few, if any, American cities can match Boston's Irish pride. Come Paddy's Day, pubs host live Irish bands and increasingly raucous crowds as the Guinness and the Shamrock-green ale flow freely. The South Boston St. Patrick's Day Parade, with its famous drum corps, starts off from Broadway "T" station.

St. Patrick's Day Parade

9 Dine Out Boston

For one to two weeks in March and August, more than 100 restaurants in Boston, Cambridge, and neighboring suburbs offer bargain, fixed-price lunch and dinner menus. Locals look forward to, and make the most of, the opportunity to sample new restaurants, so it is wise to make reservations.

10 Lilac Sunday

While the Arnold Arboretum (see p131) includes 4,463 species of flora, one plant deserves particular celebration. When its 500 lilac plants are at their fragrant, color-washed peak, garden enthusiasts arrive in droves for a May Sunday of picnics, folk dancing, and walking tours of the lilac collections.

TOP 10 SPORTING TRADITIONS

Boston Celtics in action

1 Boston Marathon
3rd Mon Apr ▪ 617 236 1652
The country's oldest marathon.

2 Head of the Charles Regatta
3rd Sat & Sun Oct ▪ 617 868 6200
Rowing crews race down the Charles while the banks teem with onlookers.

3 Red Sox vs Yankees
617 267 1700
The most heated rivalry in US sports flares up every time the Yanks visit Fenway Park (see p117).

4 Boston Celtics
617 624 1000
The Celts keep basketball playoff dreams alive at the TD Garden.

5 Boston Bruins
617 624 1000
Crowds cheer this ice hockey team at the TD Garden.

6 New England Patriots
800 543 1776
Gillette Stadium is the home of the Patriots, three-time Super Bowl champs.

7 Harvard vs Yale
617 495 3454
These Ivy League football teams butt helmets every other fall.

8 Beanpot Hockey Tournament
617 624 1000
Every February Boston's top collegiate hockey teams play each other.

9 New England Revolution
800 543 1776
The local entry in Major League Soccer is an annual playoff threat at Gillette Stadium.

10 New Year's Day Swim
The "L Street Brownies" swimming club take a dip in Boston Harbor every Jan 1.

Boston
Area by Area

Brick-built row houses in
Boston's historic North End

📶 Beacon Hill

With its elegant, 19th-century row houses, quaint grocers, pricey antiques shops, and hidden gardens, Beacon Hill screams "old money" like no other area in Boston. That some of the city's most exorbitant apartment rentals can still be found here suggests it will remain an enclave of exclusivity for years to come. Yet throughout the 19th century and well into the 20th, this inimitably charming neighborhood was

Nichols House Museum exhibit

a veritable checkerboard of ethnicities and earning groups – segregated though they were. Little of Beacon Hill's diversity has survived its inevitable gentrification, but visitors can still experience the neighborhood's myriad pasts inside its opulent mansions and humble schoolhouses, and along its enchanting cobblestone streets.

Louisburg Square residences

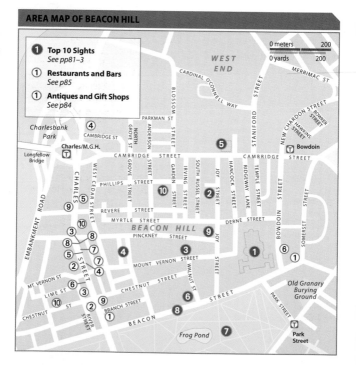

AREA MAP OF BEACON HILL

1. **Top 10 Sights**
   See pp81–3

1. **Restaurants and Bars**
   See p85

1. **Antiques and Gift Shops**
   See p84

Gleaming dome and elegant frontage of the Massachusetts State House

1 Massachusetts State House

MAP P3 ▪ 24 Beacon St ▪ 617 727 3676 ▪ Tours 10am–3:30pm Mon–Fri (reservations recommended) ▪ www.sec.state.ma.us/trs

A 200-year-old codfish, a stained-glass image of a Native American in a grass skirt, and a 23-carat gold dome crowned with a pine cone – such are the curious eccentricities that distinguish Beacon Hill's most prestigious address *(see p15).*

2 Museum of African American History

MAP N2 ▪ 46 Joy St ▪ 617 725 0022 ▪ Open 10am–4pm Mon–Sat ▪ Adm ▪ www.maah.org

Based in the African Meeting House (the oldest extant black church in the US) and the adjoining Abiel Smith School (the nation's first publicly funded grammar school for African-American children), the MAAH offers a look into the daily life of free, pre-Civil War African-Americans. The meeting house was a political and religious center for Boston's African-American community and it was here that abolitionists such as Frederick Douglass and William Lloyd Garrison delivered anti-slavery addresses in the mid-19th century. The museum has successfully preserved their legacy and that of countless others through its wide and fascinating range of workshops, exhibitions, and special events.

3 Nichols House Museum

MAP N3 ▪ 55 Mount Vernon St ▪ 617 227 6993 ▪ Open Apr–Oct: 11am–4pm Tue–Sat; Nov–Mar: 11am–4pm Thu–Sat ▪ Adm ▪ www.nicholshousemuseum.org

An 1804 Charles Bulfinch design, 55 Mount Vernon is one of the earliest examples of residential architecture on Beacon Hill. Rose Nichols, the house's principal occupant for 75 years, bequeathed her home to the city as a museum, providing a glimpse of late 19th- and early 20th-century life on the Hill. A pioneering force for women in the arts and sciences, Nichols gained fame through her authoritative writings on landscape architecture and philanthropic projects.

4 Louisburg Square

MAP N3

Cobblestone streets, a genteel little gated park, and a hefty dose of Boston Brahmin cachet make this tight block of town houses the city's most exclusive patch of real estate. Modeled after the traditional residential squares of London in 1826, the square was named in remembrance of the 1745 Battle of Louisburg in modern-day Quebec.

5 Harrison Gray Otis House

MAP N2 ▪ 141 Cambridge St ▪ 617 994 5920 ▪ Open Mar–Nov: 11am–5pm Wed–Sun; Dec–Feb: 11am–5pm Fri–Sun ▪ Adm ▪ www.historicnewengland.org

One of the principal developers of Beacon Hill, Harrison Gray Otis *(see p44)* served in the Massachusetts legislature and gained a reputation for living the high life in this 1796 Bulfinch-designed manse. Like a post-revolutionary Gatsby, Otis ensured his parties were the social events of the year. After falling into disrepair, the property was acquired in 1916 by the historical preservation society and has been restored to its original grandeur.

6 Parkman House

MAP N3 ▪ 33 Beacon St
▪ Closed to the public

George Parkman – once a prominent physician at Harvard Medical School – lived in this house during the mid 19th century. In 1849, in one of the most sensationalized murder cases in US history, Parkman was killed by a faculty member, Dr. John Webster, over a financial dispute. Both the crime and its aftermath were grisly – the ensuing trial saw the inclusion of dental records as evidence for the first time. The house is now a city-owned meeting center.

BLACK HERITAGE TRAIL

By and large the Paul Reveres and John Adamses of this world have monopolized the history books. As a refreshing counterpoint, the Black Heritage Trail posits that black Bostonians, despite their marginalized histories, have played an indispensable role in the city's development. The trail illustrates this point at every turn, taking visitors past the homes and businesses of some of Boston's most influential black Americans. Tours leave from the Shaw Memorial daily in summer, Mon–Sat in fall. Call 24 hours in advance for times and to book (617 742 5415; www.nps.gov/boaf).

7 Boston Common

The oldest city park in the country, the Common is a popular gathering place for outdoor concerts, public protests, picnics in summer and, in the winter, ice-skating on Frog Pond *(see pp18–19)*.

8 Beacon Street

MAP N3 ▪ Boston Athenaeum: 10½ Beacon St ▪ 617 227 0270 ▪ Open 9am–8pm Mon–Thu, 9am–5:30pm Fri, 9am–4pm Sat, 12pm–4pm Sun; tours 3pm Tue & Thu, by reservation

Beacon Street, in the blocks between Somerset and Brimmer streets, features the National Historic

George Washington statue in Boston Gardens

Boston Athenaeum library

Landmark Boston Athenaeum, one of the oldest independent libraries in the country, housed in a sumptuous building containing a collection of over 600,000 titles. Also here are the Massachusetts State House *(see p15)*, Parkman House *(see p82)*, and the Third Harrison Otis House, at 45 Beacon St, considered architect Charles Bulfinch's finest Federal-style house. The facade of the former Bull and Finch Pub at 84 Beacon St is famed as the exterior of the bar in the TV show *Cheers*.

9 George Middleton House
MAP N3 ■ 5–7 Pinckney St
■ **Closed to the public**

The oldest remaining private residence on Beacon Hill built by African-Americans is a highlight of the Black Heritage Trail. George Middleton, a Revolutionary War veteran, commissioned the house's construction soon after the war. Legend has it that he commanded an all-black company dubbed the "Bucks of America."

10 Boston's Center for Jewish Culture
MAP N2 ■ 13–18 Phillips St ■ 617 523 2324 ■ Call for hours ■ www. vilnashul.com

The Vilna Shul testifies to the area's former vibrancy as Boston's first predominantly Jewish quarter. The congregation was founded in 1903 by immigrants who came from Vilna, Lithuania. It is now a center of Jewish culture with programs and exhibits.

BEACON HILL BY DAY

Savenor's Market / Charles/M.G.H. Station / Museum of African American History / Panificio Bakery / Good / Charles Street / Massachusetts State House / The Sevens Ale House / Paramount / Shaw Memorial / Black Heritage Trail / Bull and Finch Pub / Boston Common

► MORNING

Take the "T" to the Charles Street/Massachusetts General Hospital stop and exit onto Charles Street. Enjoy a light breakfast at **Panificio Bakery** (144 Charles St) where the scones and muffins are out of this world. Then continue along Charles Street and turn right onto Beacon Street for a glimpse of the former **Bull and Finch Pub** – the bar that inspired the TV show *Cheers*. Continue up Beacon to the **Massachusetts State House** *(see p81)* for a free 45-minute tour; times vary. Afterward, cross the road to the Shaw Memorial, where a National Park ranger-led **Black Heritage Trail** tour departs at noon during summer. The trail provides an excellent survey of the area's architectural styles as well as its black culture sites, and ends at the **Museum of African American History** *(see p81)*.

AFTERNOON

Walk back down the hill to Charles Street for a fortifying late lunch. Weather permitting, stock up on fresh fruit, a crusty baguette, and a sampling of imported cheeses at the charming **Savenor's Market** (160 Charles St) and have a picnic on the Common. Or, for inexpensive, diner-style American fare (meatloaf and fruit pies), try the **Paramount** (44 Charles St). After lunch, peruse the sleek accessories, art, and design at **Good** (133 Charles St) and spend the afternoon browsing Charles Street's antique shops *(see p84)*. Round the day off with a pint at **The Sevens Ale House** *(see p85)*.

See map on p80 ←

Antiques and Gift Shops

Devonia Antiques

1 Devonia Antiques
MAP M3 ■ 15 Charles St
■ Closed Tue

Fine antique English porcelain and American and European stemware. Thousands of museum-quality and collector items are on display, including hand-painted cabinet plates, and individual pieces, as well as complete dinner services.

2 Eugene Galleries
MAP M3 ■ 76 Charles St

This shop has an excellent and fascinating selection of antique books, maps, and prints, including many depicting the development and history of Boston.

3 Beacon Hill Chocolates
MAP M3 ■ 91 Charles St
■ Closed Sun

Handmade boxes decorated with vintage Boston scenes are ideal for a gift assortment of artisan chocolates. Don't miss the signature swirl of Caramel Sushi.

Beacon Hill Chocolates

4 20th Century Limited
MAP M3 ■ 73 Charles St

This shop specializes in vintage designer costume jewelry and estate jewelry, but there's also handsome 1950s barware, vintage clothing accessories, and other collectibles.

5 Boston Antiques Company
MAP M3 ■ 119 Charles St

Twelve dealers operate in this lower-level space filled with treasures including Asian antiques, militaria, Impressionist landscape paintings, and much more.

6 Blackstone's of Beacon Hill
MAP M3 ■ 46 Charles St

This is the place to go for unique Boston-themed gifts such as *Make Way for Ducklings* pillows and ornaments, as well as high-quality Fenway Park mugs.

7 Elegant Findings
MAP M3 ■ 89 Charles St
■ Closed Tue, Wed & Sun

This intimate shop specializes in museum-quality, hand-painted 19th-century porcelain from all over Europe. You'll also find marble statuary, exquisite linens, and fine period furniture.

8 Upstairs Downstairs
MAP M3 ■ 93 Charles St

This cozy shop places a refreshing emphasis on affordability and function. Everything from mahogany four-poster beds to *belle époque* opera glasses is on display.

9 Marika's Antiques
MAP M3 ■ 130 Charles St ■ Closed Sun & Mon

Packed to its dusty rafters with oil paintings, tarnished silverware, and mismatched china – nothing quite beats that thrill of discovery you'll find here.

10 Black Ink
MAP M3 ■ 101 Charles St

Labeled "unexpected necessities" by the owners, merchandise here ranges from four-way rubber bands to Weck canning jars to rubber stamps (hence the name).

Restaurants and Bars

1 Mooo
MAP P3 ■ 15 Beacon St ■ 617 670 2515 ■ $$$

Mooo specializes in extraordinary beef and classic accompaniments at expense-account prices. The wine list includes many stellar names.

2 Bin 26 Enoteca
MAP M2 ■ 26 Charles St ■ 617 723 5939 ■ $$$

Neighborhood wine bar with an Italian accent, offering a range of small dishes for sharing along with 60 wines by the glass.

3 Figs
MAP M3 ■ 42 Charles St ■ 617 742 3447 ■ Closed L Mon–Fri ■ $

This popular spot created by local celeb-chef Todd English specializes in pizza with inventive toppings such as artichoke, caramelized leeks, goat's cheese, and basil oil.

4 Scampo
MAP F3 ■ Liberty Hotel, 215 Charles St ■ 617 536 2100 ■ $$$

Bold design and Italian cuisine with a twist graces the first floor of the swank Liberty Hotel.

5 The Sevens Ale House
MAP M3 ■ 77 Charles St

The epitome of a local Boston bar: dark wood, slightly surly staff, amiable patrons, a dartboard, and a rudimentary pub menu.

6 21st Amendment
MAP G3 ■ 150 Bowdoin St

This neighborhood pub near the State House is a classy spot for legislators and movers and shakers to indulge in a tipple or two.

7 Lala Rokh
MAP N3 ■ 97 Mount Vernon St ■ 617 720 5511 ■ Closed L Sat & Sun ■ $$

Authentic Persian cuisine is served in this casual spot. Citrus-based glazes and relishes give meats amazing piquant flavor.

8 Artù
MAP M3 ■ 89 Charles St ■ 617 227 9023 ■ Closed L Sun & Mon ■ $$

Tuscan specialties such as *porchetta*, lamb cutlets, spicy seafood, and roasted veggies come sizzling off the grill straight to your table.

Beacon Hill Bistro

9 Beacon Hill Bistro
MAP M3 ■ 25 Charles St ■ 617 723 1133 ■ Open for brunch Sat & Sun, closed L Sat & Sun ■ $$$

This kitchen (in the Beacon Hill Hotel) puts an American stamp on French bistro cuisine to great effect.

10 75 Chestnut
MAP M3 ■ 75 Chestnut St ■ 617 227 2175 ■ Closed L except Sat & Sun brunch ■ $$

This converted town house offers one of Beacon Hill's most popular drinking and dining hangouts for brunch and dinner. The menu offers affordable American bistro dishes.

See map on p80

TOP 10 Back Bay

Boston Public Library

The easily navigated grid of streets in Back Bay bears little resemblance to the labyrinthine lanes around Downtown and the North End. In the mid-1800s Back Bay was filled in to accommodate Boston's mushrooming population and, by the late 1800s, the area had become a vibrant, upscale neighborhood. Home to many of Boston's wealthiest families, the area was characterized by lavish houses, grand churches, and bustling commercial zones. Many of the original buildings stand intact, providing an exquisite 19th-century backdrop for today's pulsing nightlife, world-class shopping, and sumptuous dining.

AREA MAP OF BACK BAY

1. **Top 10 Sights**
   See pp87–9
1. **Restaurants**
   See p93
1. **Newbury Shops**
   See p91
1. **Art Galleries**
   See p90
1. **Nightclubs and Bars**
   See p92

1 Trinity Church

When I. M. Pei's 60-story John Hancock Tower was completed in 1976, Bostonians feared that Trinity Church would be overshadowed by its gleaming upstart neighbor. Yet H. H. Richardson's masterpiece, dedicated in 1877, remains just as vital to Copley Square, and as beautiful, as it was on its opening day (see pp32–3).

2 The Esplanade
MAP M3

The perfect setting for a leisurely bike ride, an invigorating jog, or a lazy afternoon of soaking up the sun, the Esplanade is one of the city's most popular green spaces. This ribbon of green hugging the Charles' riverbanks was inspired by Venetian canals.

View from the Esplanade

July 4th (see p76) at the Esplanade's Hatch Shell concert venue brings the world-famous Boston Pops Orchestra along with thousands of revelers to enjoy the incomparable mix of music, good cheer, and awe-inspiring fireworks. Use caution if on the esplanade at night.

3 Boston Public Library
MAP L5 ■ 700 Boylston St ■ 617 536 5400 ■ Open 9am–9pm Mon–Thu, 9am–5pm Fri & Sat, 1–5pm Sun (Jun–Sep: closed Sun) ■ Tours: 2:30pm Mon, 6pm Tue & Thu, 11am Wed, Fri & Sat, 2pm Sun ■ www.bpl.org

Although this McKim, Mead, & White-designed building went up in 1895, the Boston Public Library was actually founded in 1848 and is the oldest publicly funded library in the country. The interior's Greco-Roman style cues lavish use of marble, and John Singer Sargent's powerful Judaism and Christianity mural sequence clearly illustrates how valued public education was when the library was constructed. Guided tours offer insight into the building's architecture and history.

4 Newbury Street

Over the years, Back Bay's most famous street has proven to be amazingly adaptable, with fashion boutiques blending seamlessly into their mid-19th-century brownstone environs. This is the liveliest, most eclectic street in Boston: a babble of languages, skater punks alongside catwalk models, and delivery trucks and Ferraris jockeying for the same parking space (see pp24–5).

⑤ Gibson House Museum
MAP M4 ▪ 137 Beacon St ▪ 617 267 6338 ▪ Tours 1pm, 2pm, & 3pm Wed–Sun ▪ Adm ▪ www.thegibsonhouse.org

One of the first private residences to be built in Back Bay (c.1859), Gibson House remains beautifully intact. The house has been preserved as a monument to the era, thanks largely to the efforts of its final resident (the grandson of the well-to-do woman who built the house). So frozen in time does this house appear that you might feel like you're intruding on someone's inner sanctum, and an earlier age. Highlights of the tour include some elegant porcelain dinnerware, 18th-century heirloom jewelry, and exquisite black walnut woodwork throughout the house.

⑥ Prudential Center
MAP K6 ▪ 800 Boylston St ▪ 617 236 3100 ▪ Open 10am–9pm Mon–Sat, 11am–8pm Sun

Although it's difficult to imagine, the Prudential Tower's 52 stories seem dwarfed by the huge swath of street-level shops and restaurants that constitute the Prudential Center. With its indoor shopping mall, eateries, supermarket, cluster of residential towers, and massive convention center, the Prudential Center is like a self-contained city within a city. For a jaw-dropping view of Boston, visit the Skywalk on the tower's 50th level (see p51), or the Top of the Hub Lounge (see p92), two floors above.

Commonwealth Avenue

⑦ Commonwealth Avenue
MAP J5–L4

With its leafy pedestrian mall and *belle époque*-inspired architecture, Commonwealth Avenue aptly deserves its comparison to *les rues parisiennes*. A morning jog on the mall is a popular pastime, as is the occasional picnic or afternoon snooze on a bench. Highlights include Boston's First Baptist Church (110 Commonwealth; closed to non-worshipers) and the pedestrian mall's stately statues, including the William Lloyd Garrison bronze, sculpted by local artist Anne Whitney.

⑧ Christian Science Center
MAP K6 ▪ 175 Huntington Ave ▪ 617 450 7000 ▪ Library open 10am–4pm Tue–Sun ▪ Adm ▪ www.marybakereddylibrary.org

While believers head for the Romanesque-Byzantine basilica, the library (entered from Massachusetts Avenue) emphasizes inspirational facets of the life of the founder (see pp44–5) rather than church doctrine.

Christian Science Center and the Prudential Center

The Mapparium, a walk-through stained-glass globe with 1935 political boundaries, remains the most popular exhibit *(see p48)*. Peer into the newsroom of the *Christian Science Monitor*. Outside, a 670-ft (204-m) reflecting pool, designed by I. M. Pei, is lined with begonias, marigolds, and columbines. The café is a good spot for lunch.

⑨ Berklee Performance Center

MAP J6 ▪ 136 Massachusetts Ave ▪ 617 266 7455 ▪ Check website for details of concerts and performances: www.berklee.edu/BPC

The largest independent music school in the world, Berklee was founded in 1945. The college has produced a number of world-renowned jazz, rock, and pop stars, including Quincy Jones, Melissa Etheridge, Kevin Eubanks, Jan Hammer, and Branford Marsalis. The state-of-the-art performance center hosts special events including concerts, plays, and film screenings.

⑩ Copley Square

MAP L5

Named after John Singleton Copley, the renowned 18th-century Boston painter, Copley Square is surrounded by some of the city's most striking architectural gems, notably Trinity Church and the Boston Public Library. A hub of activities, the bustling square hosts weekly farmers' markets, concerts, and folk dance shows in summer. The BosTix booth sells discounted tickets for theater, music, and dance performances.

EXPLORING BACK BAY

[Map diagram with labels: Public Garden, Fresh, Ben & Jerry's, Trident Booksellers, Boston Public Library, Trinity Church, Parish Café, Copley Plaza Hotel, Prudential Center, Top of the Hub Lounge]

▶ AFTERNOON

Grab a patio table at the **Parish Café** *(see p71)* and enjoy an inventive sandwich while gazing out onto the **Public Garden** (see pp18–19). Stroll one block over to **Newbury Street** (see pp24–5) and take in the impressive contemporary art galleries concentrated between Arlington and Dartmouth streets. Then cross back over to Boylston at Dartmouth and sit for a while inside **Trinity Church** *(see pp32–3)* where La Farge's stained-glass windows top an inexhaustible list of highlights. And while you're in an aesthetics-appreciating mood, traverse St. James Place to the **Copley Plaza Hotel** and lounge for a few moments in the ornate, Versailles-esque lobby. Next, cross Dartmouth to the **Boston Public Library** *(see p87)* and admire John Singer Sargent's gorgeous murals.

Now it's time to warm up your credit card, so head back to **Newbury Street** for a dizzying shopping spree. Turn left onto Newbury for Boston-only boutiques such as **Fresh** *(see p91)* and **Trident Booksellers** *(see p91)*. Pause for a reinvigorating fruit smoothie or thick frappé at **Ben & Jerry's** (174 Newbury St). At Massachusetts Avenue, turn left, then left again onto Boylston and continue to the **Prudential Center** for name-brand shopping – you'll find Saks Fifth Avenue, Neiman Marcus, and the like. Cap it all off with a bracing-cold cocktail and smooth jazz at the 52nd-floor **Top of the Hub Lounge** *(see p92)*, where you can soak in Boston's skyline – and, with any luck, a dazzling sunset.

See map on pp86–7 ←

Art Galleries

1 Robert Klein
MAP M5 ■ 38 Newbury St
■ 617 267 7997 ■ Closed Sun & Mon

Everybody who's anybody in photography vies for space at Robert Klein. Past coups include shows by Annie Leibovitz and Herb Ritts.

2 Copley Society of Art
MAP L5 ■ 158 Newbury St
■ 617 536 5049 ■ Closed Mon

With a commitment to exhibiting works by promising New England artists, this non-profit organization has been providing young artists with that crucial first break since 1879.

3 International Poster Gallery
MAP K5 ■ 205 Newbury St
■ 617 375 0076

Arguably the most fun – albeit the most populist – gallery on Newbury St, the IPG stocks vintage posters advertising films, travel, food, and sports.

4 Arden Gallery
MAP L5 ■ 129 Newbury St
■ 617 247 0610 ■ Closed Sun

This contemporary art gallery focuses on original paintings and sculpture, including bronze and other metals. It showcases up-and-coming abstract and realist artists.

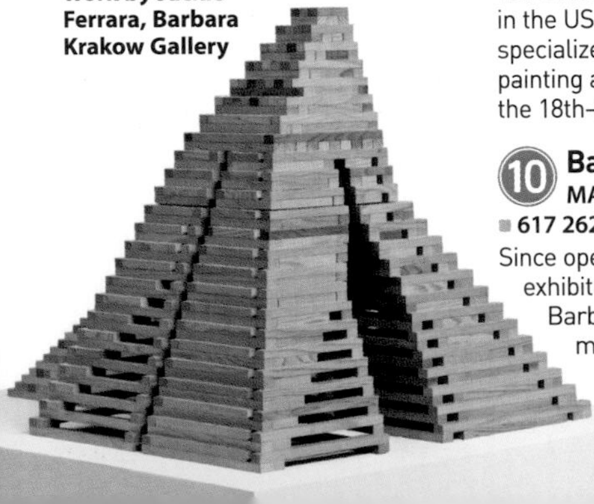

Work by Jackie Ferrara, Barbara Krakow Gallery

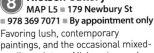

5 Society of Arts and Crafts
MAP L5 ■ 175 Newbury St
■ 617 266 1810 ■ Closed Sun & Mon

Devoted to art in craft media, this 1897 pioneer of artisanship sells a wide variety of studio crafts. Jewelry and ceramics also available.

6 Alpha Gallery
MAP M5 ■ 37 Newbury St
■ 617 536 4465 ■ Closed Sun & Mon

Founded in 1967 to showcase contemporary artists from Boston, Alpha now covers the country and features modern masters.

7 Gallery NAGA
MAP M5 ■ 67 Newbury St ■ 617 267 9060 ■ Closed Sun & Mon; Jul & Aug

Representing some of New England's most regarded artists, NAGA is possibly Newbury's best contemporary art gallery.

International Poster Gallery print

8 Nielsen Gallery
MAP L5 ■ 179 Newbury St
■ 978 369 7071 ■ By appointment only

Favoring lush, contemporary paintings, and the occasional mixed-media sculpture, Nielsen is popular among Boston's art cognoscenti.

9 Vose Galleries
MAP K5 ■ 238 Newbury St
■ 617 536 6176 ■ Closed Sun & Mon

The oldest family-owned art gallery in the US (open since 1841), Vose specializes in American realist painting and works on paper from the 18th–20th centuries.

10 Barbara Krakow Gallery
MAP M5 ■ 10 Newbury St
■ 617 262 4490 ■ Closed Sun & Mon

Since opening in 1964 with an exhibition of Ellsworth Kelly prints, Barbara Krakow's keen judgment of contemporary art has earned her many fans – and customers.

Homegrown Newbury Shops

1 Johnny Cupcakes
MAP K6 ■ 279 Newbury St

This boutique specializes in limited-edition crossbones-and-cupcake T-shirts. The joke continues with bakery case displays, aprons on the staff, and the smell of cake batter in the air.

2 Trident Booksellers & Café
MAP K6 ■ 338 Newbury St

Trident is popular for its delicious, healthy sandwiches, strong coffee concoctions, and arguably the best-informed book and magazine selections in the city.

Newbury Comics

3 Newbury Comics
MAP J6 ■ 332 Newbury St

Generally undercutting the chain stores on CDs, Newbury Comics delivers value along with a stellar selection of rare import CDs and a growing range of exclusive, rare and vintage vinyl, as well as concert videos, and the latest comics.

4 Fresh
MAP L5 ■ 121 Newbury St

Chic grooming products for men and women, many of them based on such natural products as sugar (for face and body skin polish), clay (masks and lotions), and soy (facial cleaning gel).

5 Hempest
MAP K5 ■ 207 Newbury St

A true believer in the superiority of hemp as something to put on rather than inhale, Hempest showcases chic and casual styles fashioned from this environmentally friendly fiber.

6 Boston Olive Oil Company
MAP K5 ■ 253 Newbury St

This family-owned shop offers more than 60 premium varieties of Extra Virgin olive oil and balsamic vinegars.

7 Second Time Around
MAP L5 ■ 176 Newbury St

Before blowing your budget on that Chanel handbag, take a peek at Second Time Around, where used designer clothing and accessories get a second lease on life. Think head-to-toe Versace for a mere $100.

8 Condom World
MAP J6 ■ 332 Newbury St

Check your inhibitions at this sub-terranean boutique's door. While male anatomy-shaped ketchup dispensers deserve a laugh, some of the sex toys toward the back might raise some eyebrows.

9 Simon Pearce
MAP F4 ■ 103 Newbury St

Fine blown glass and handmade pottery from this eponymous Irish designer and artist creates tableware with an upscale touch. Pearce signatures include classic goblets and other stemware.

10 Deluca's Back Bay Market
MAP K5 ■ 239 Newbury St

This old world-style corner market stocks fabulous produce, chilled beer, ready-made sandwiches, and imported delights of all kinds.

See map on pp86–7

Nightclubs and Bars

View over the city from the Top of the Hub Lounge

1 Top of the Hub Lounge
MAP K6 ■ Prudential Tower, 800 Boylston St

Talk about a view: 52 stories above Back Bay, this bar dazzles with sweeping views, live jazz, deliciously sophisticated lounge food menu, and a wicked gin martini.

2 City Bar
MAP L5 ■ 65 Exeter St

The epitome of a stylish yet discreet hotel lounge, City Bar serves up designer cocktails and light snacks.

3 Kings
MAP J6 ■ 10 Scotia St

The 1950s were never so cool as they seem at this retro-styled lounge, pool hall, and bowling alley buried downstairs next to the Hynes Convention Center.

4 Storyville
MAP F5 ■ 94 Exeter St ■ Closed Sun–Tue

Speakeasy meets nightclub at this lounge which serves hip bar food such as short rib casserole, and snazzy cocktails.

5 Whiskey's
MAP K6 ■ 885 Boylston St

Be sure to have ID in hand before putting pint to mouth at this lively bar. It's full of hard-drinking collegiate types, who arrive around 6pm and stay until last call.

6 Bar at the Taj
MAP F4 ■ 15 Arlington St ■ Closes 11:30pm, 12:30am Fri & Sat

Boston's elite have been socializing at this elegant room facing the Public Garden since the 1920s.

7 The Pour House
MAP K6 ■ 907 Boylston St

Cheap, hearty pub grub and occasional drink specials lure college kids to this two-story bar and grill. It's loud, it's crowded, and you're bound to make a friend or two.

8 Bukowski Tavern
MAP K6 ■ 50 Dalton St

A beer drinker's paradise, Bukowski counts 100 varieties of the beverage. Its primary patrons are a professional crowd during the day and young hipsters at night.

9 Lolita Cocina & Tequila Bar
MAP L5 ■ 271 Dartmouth St

There's always a festive mood at this trendy, Gothic-styled bar. Choose from the long list of specialty tequilas, accompanied by Mexican food.

10 Bristol Bar
MAP N4 ■ 200 Boylston St ■ Closes 1am

Sharing room with the excellent Bristol Lounge, this sophisticated bar in the Four Seasons hotel charms visitors with its signature martinis.

Restaurants

PRICE CATEGORIES
For a three-course meal for one with half a bottle of wine (or equivalent meal), taxes, and extra charges.

$ under $40 $$ $40–$60 $$$ over $60

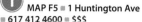

1 Sorellina
MAP F5 ▪ 1 Huntington Ave ▪ 617 412 4600 ▪ $$$
Regional Italian food with a contemporary spin is accompanied by a range of great wines and served up in a sophisticated dining room.

2 L'Espalier
MAP K6 ▪ 774 Boylston St ▪ 617 262 3023 ▪ $$$
New England ingredients combine with high-style modern French technique to create memorable, luxury dining.

3 Deuxave
MAP E5 ▪ 371 Commonwealth Ave ▪ 617 517 5915 ▪ Closed L ▪ $$$
Elegant contemporary dining ranges from local lobster and scallops to caramelized onion ravioli. In summer, outside seating is available.

4 Douzo
MAP L6 ▪ 131 Dartmouth St ▪ 617 859 8886 ▪ $$$
The serene setting of rich, dark wood and high ceilings makes one of the city's best sushi restaurants something of a Zen experience.

5 Post 390
MAP M5 ▪ 406 Stuart St ▪ 617 399 0015 ▪ Closed L Sat & Sun ▪ $$$
This urban tavern near the South End border is a comfortable meeting spot, with three fireplaces, two bars, and an open kitchen on two levels.

6 Mistral
MAP M6 ▪ 223 Columbus Ave ▪ 617 867 9300 ▪ $$$
Delectable French-Mediterranean dishes and an excellent wine list make Mistral an ideal dining venue.

7 Uni
MAP J5 ▪ 370A Commonwealth Ave ▪ 617 536 7200 ▪ Closed L & Mon ▪ $$$
Chef Ken Oringer presents his own interpretation of contemporary Japanese cuisine at this fine-dining restaurant in the Eliot Hotel.

8 Brasserie Jo
MAP K6 ▪ 120 Huntington Ave ▪ 617 425 3240 ▪ $$
Bustling Brasserie Jo captures the *savoir faire* of 1940s Paris. Relish hearty French classics like steak roquefort.

9 Erbaluce
MAP G5 ▪ 69 Church St ▪ 617 426 6969 ▪ $$$
Chef Charles Draghi brings French technical finesse to north Italian cuisine with a menu that changes nightly. Excellent, all-Italian wine list.

10 Grill 23
MAP M5 ▪ 161 Berkeley St ▪ 617 542 2255 ▪ Closed L ▪ $$$
Grill 23 harkens back to the days of exclusive, Prohibition-era supper clubs. Prime aged beef with an inventive spin is served in a sumptuously classic interior.

Entrance to Grill 23

See map on pp86–7

🔟 North End and the Waterfront

Old North Church road marker

The North End is Boston's Italian village, where one feast day blends into the next all summer as the great-grandchildren of the original immigrants celebrate the music, food, and dolce vita of the old country. Yet the North End predates its Italian inhabitants and the neighborhood is in fact the oldest in Boston. The area along the waterfront bristles with condo developments on former shipping piers, which lead south to the bustle of Long, Central, and Rowes wharves. Boston was born by the sea and it is now reclaiming its waterfront as a vital center for business and pleasure.

AREA MAP OF NORTH END AND THE WATERFRONT

North End

0 meters 150
0 yards 150

1 Top 10 Sights
See pp95–7

1 Restaurants and Bars
See p99

1 Italian Bakeries and Grocers
See p98

0 meters 400
0 yards 400

1 Copp's Hill Burying Ground

MAP Q1 ▪ Entrance on Hull St ▪ 617 635 4505 ▪ Open 9am–5pm daily ▪ No DA

Trace the history of Boston on the thousands of tombstones here, from the mean-spirited Mather family, theocrats who ruled the early city, to the valiant patriots slain in the fight for freedom. In the Battle of Bunker Hill *(see p14)*, the British, who occupied the city in 1775, manned a battery from this site and fired on neighboring Charlestown. There are sweeping views of the harbor.

2 Old North Church

MAP Q1 ▪ 193 Salem St ▪ 617 523 6676 ▪ Open Jun–Oct: 9am–6pm daily (shorter hours off-season) ▪ Donation ▪ www.oldnorth.com

An active Episcopal congregation still worships at Boston's oldest church, officially known as Christ Church (1723). It was here, in 1775, that sexton Robert Newman hung two lanterns in the belfry to warn horseback messenger Paul Revere of British troop movements, an event commemorated by a bronze plaque in the street outside *(see p14)*.

Paul Revere House

3 Paul Revere House

MAP Q1 ▪ 19 North Sq ▪ 617 523 2338 ▪ Open mid-Apr–Oct: 9:30am–5:15pm daily; Nov–mid Apr: 9:30am–4:15pm daily (closed Mon Jan–Mar) ▪ Adm ▪ Limited DA ▪ www.paulreverehouse.org

Home to Paul Revere for 30 years, this 17th-century clapboard house is the only surviving home of any of Boston's revolutionary heroes. It provides an intriguing glimpse into the domestic life of Revere's family with displays of their furniture and possessions, including silverwork made by Revere, who was highly regarded as a metalsmith. Well-trained staff tell the tale of Revere's legendary midnight ride *(see p14)*.

4 Hanover Street

MAP Q22

Originally built in the 17th century to link the shipping wharves to Dock Square (now Faneuil Hall Market-place; *see p101*), Hanover Street was widened in 1870 to accommodate the busy flow of commerce. Today, as the North End's principal artery, with cafés and eateries aplenty, it is the place to come for a slice of the action.

5 New England Aquarium

MAP R3

Now the centerpiece of the down-town waterfront development, the aquarium's construction in the 1960s paved the way for the revitalization of Boston Harbor as a whole. Seals cavort in a tank in front of the sleek modern structure *(see pp38–9)*.

Old North Church

Exterior of the Children's Museum

6 Children's Museum

Educators at this ground-breaking interactive museum for kids pioneered some of the features now found in similar facilities around the world, including giant soap bubbles and complex rampways for marbles *(see p50).*

7 Institute of Contemporary Art

100 Northern Ave ▪ 617 478 3100 ▪ Open 10am–5pm Tue, Wed, Sat & Sun, 10am–9pm Thu & Fri ▪ Adm ▪ www.icaboston.org

The ICA was founded in 1936 and reopened in its modern landmark structure on Fan Pier in 2006. The striking glass, wood, and steel building, designed by Diller Scofidio + Renfro, is cantilevered over the HarborWalk and provides dramatic views. The ICA promotes cutting-edge art and focuses on 21st-century work. There is also a program of performing arts and other events, with waterfront concerts in summer.

Harborside setting of the Boston Tea Party Ships and Museum

FORAGING FOR FORMAGGIO

Italian food, wine, and culture expert Michele Topor has lived in the North End for four decades. Her tour of the local markets on Wednesday and Saturday (10am, 1pm, 2pm, 5pm), and Friday (10am, 1pm, 3pm, 6pm) includes tastings and insights on local restaurants. To reserve a place, contact Boston Food Tours: 855 249 1163, www.bostonfoodtours.com.

8 Boston Tea Party Ships and Museum

MAP R5 ▪ Congress St Bridge ▪ 617 338 1773 ▪ Open 10am–5pm daily ▪ Adm ▪ www.bostonteapartyship.com

The historic occasion known as the Boston Tea Party, when patriots dressed as Native Americans and threw a consignment of English tea overboard to protest against the Stamp Tax of 1773, proved to be a catalyst of the American Revolution *(see p14).* The Boston Tea Party ships are replicas of two of the three vessels that were relieved of their cargo that fateful December night. Costumed storytellers recount events in rousing detail, and visitors can board one of the vessels and even participate in a re-enactment of the destruction of the tea. In the museum is one of two tea crates known to have survived from the incident, while Abigail's Tea Room serves up a nice "cuppa."

9 Rose Kennedy Greenway

MAP P1 ■ www.rosekennedy
greenway.org

The Greenway is a ribbon of organic,
contemporary parkland through the
heart of Boston, where visitors and
locals laze on the lawns, cool off in
the fountains, buy lunch at one of the
affordable food trucks, and enjoy free
Wi-Fi. There's a charming carousel
featuring local hand-carved wildlife,
with a cod, lobster, rabbit, and more.
Artworks include the Harbor Fog
water sculpture, near Rowes
Wharf, which evokes the sea with
fog, light, and sound, as well as
installations that change every year.
Colorful garden plants punctuate
the walkways.

Rose Kennedy Greenway

10 St. Stephen's Church

MAP R1 ■ 401 Hanover St ■ 617
523 1230 ■ Open 8:30am–4:30pm
Mon–Sat, 11am Sun for worship

Renowned architect Charles Bulfinch
completely redesigned St. Stephen's
original 1714 structure in 1802–4,
and the church is the only surviving
example of his religious architecture.
Its bell was cast by Paul Revere.
The complex Neo-Classical exterior
contrasts with the open, airy, and
relatively unadorned interior. In 1862,
the Roman Catholic archdiocese
took over the church to accommodate the area's growing number
of Irish immigrants. Rose Fitzgerald,
daughter of Boston mayor and St.
Stephen's parishioner John "Honey
Fitz" Fitzgerald and mother of
President J.F. Kennedy (see p45),
is linked to the church. She was
baptized here in 1890, and her
funeral took place here in 1995.

FROM NARROW BYWAYS TO THE SEA

▶ MORNING

From the Haymarket "T," follow
Hanover Street to Richmond
Street and continue to North
Square. Stop at **Paul Revere
House** (see p95) for a glimpse
into the domestic life of the
revolutionary hero. Return to
Hanover for an espresso and
some prime people-watching
at lively **Caffè Vittoria** (see p70).
Continue up Hanover and turn
left through Paul Revere Mall
to **Old North Church** (see p95).
The bust of George Washington
inside is reputedly the world's
most accurate rendering of his
face – compare the resemblance
to a dollar bill. Then stroll up Hull
Street past **Copp's Hill Burying
Ground** (see p95) for a great view
of USS *Constitution* (see p36) and
continue to the waterfront (see
p47). Grab a bench in **Puopolo
Park** to watch a match of *bocce*.
Walk south along Commercial
Street and stop for an alfresco
waterside lunch at **Joe's American
Bar & Grill** (100 Atlantic Ave).

AFTERNOON

Resume your waterfront stroll
along the Rose Kennedy
Greenway and stop off to enjoy
the roses in the **Rose Kennedy
Rose Garden**, before whiling away
an hour or so in the **New England
Aquarium** (see pp38–9) where
highlights include the swirling
Giant Ocean Tank. Relax with a
sundowner on the patio of the
Boston Harbor Hotel (70 Rowes
Wharf) before you head to
Sportello (see p99) for dinner.

See map on p94

Italian Bakeries and Grocers

1 Mike's Pastry
MAP Q1 ■ 300 Hanover St

Large glass cases display a huge selection of cookies and *cannoli* (crunchy pastry filled with a sweet ricotta cream). Purchase a box to go, or grab a table and order a drink and a delectable pastry.

2 Salumeria Italiana
MAP Q2
■ 151 Richmond St

This neighborhood fixture is a great source of esoteric Italian canned goods and rich olive oils, as well as spicy sausages and cheeses from many Italian regions.

Modern Pastry shop sign

3 Maria's Pastry Shop
MAP Q2 ■ 46 Cross St

Run for three generations by the Merola family, Maria's is famed for its Neapolitan flaky and sweet *sfogliatelle* (filled pastry) as well as seasonal sweets, such as chocolate-allspice cookies at Christmas and marzipan lambs at Easter.

4 Polcari's Coffee Co.
MAP Q1 ■ 105 Salem St
■ Closed Sun

The premier bulk grocer in the North End, this charming store has sold fine Italian roasted coffee since 1932. It's still the best place to find spices, flours, grains, and legumes.

5 Bova's Bakery
MAP Q1 ■ 134 Salem St

Fresh bread emerges from the ovens at all hours. When the coffee shops and bars close, head to Bova's for hot sandwiches and cookies.

6 Modern Pastry
MAP Q2 ■ 257 Hanover St

The house specialties here include a rich ricotta pie, delicious florentines, and nougat, which are all made on the premises, as well as chocolate truffles from Italy. Modern makes a thinner *cannoli* shell than Mike's.

7 Monica's Mercato
MAP Q1 ■ 130 Salem St

Linked to a nearby restaurant, this *salumeria* has all the usual cheeses and sausages, but its specialties are prepared foods such as cold salads for picnics and pasta dishes for reheating.

8 V. Cirace Wine & Spirits
MAP Q2 ■ 173 North St
■ Closed Sun

The North End's most upscale seller of Italian wines and liqueurs stocks both fine wines to lay down and cheerfully youthful ones to enjoy right away.

9 Bricco Panetteria
MAP Q2 ■ 241 Hanover St

This subterranean bakery turns out amazing Italian and French breads day and night. Follow the delicious smells to find it tucked down an alley.

10 Bricco Salumeria & Pasta Shop
MAP Q2 ■ 11 Board Alley

With many varieties of fresh pasta made daily, plus sauces, pesto, grating cheeses, and a handful of hard-to-find Italian groceries, this North End takeout is ideal for stocking up a picnic basket.

Polcari's Coffee Co.

Restaurants and Bars

PRICE CATEGORIES

For a three-course meal for one with half
a bottle of wine (or equivalent meal),
taxes, and extra charges.

....

$ under $40 $$ $40–$60 $$$ over $60

1 Maurizio's
MAP Q1 ■ 364 Hanover St
■ 617 367 1123 ■ Closed Mon ■ No
DA ■ $$

This is a cozy, buzzy spot, at which
chef Maurizio Lodo draws on his
Sardinian heritage to create dishes
that often make a feature of brilliant
preparations of fish.

Neptune Oyster

2 Neptune Oyster
MAP Q1 ■ 63 Salem St ■ 617
742 3474 ■ $$$

The delicate raw bar oysters are
almost upstaged by large and bold
roasted fish and pasta dishes in this
tiny, stylish spot. Tables turn quickly.

3 Legal Harborside
The flagship of the Legal Sea
Foods chain offers three floors of
seafood heaven. Book ahead for fine
dining on level two *(see p60)*.

4 Aragosta
MAP H2 ■ 3 Battery Wharf
■ 617 994 9001 ■ $$$

Stunning waterfront views comple-
ment Mediterranean flavors and
ocean-fresh New England seafood
at the Fairmont Hotel.

5 Pizzeria Regina
MAP Q1 ■ 11½ Thatcher St
■ No DA ■ $

Founded in 1926, the original, family-
run Regina offers brick-oven, thin-
crust, old-fashioned pizza which is
far better than the pale imitations
served at its other branches.

6 Sportello
MAP I4 ■ 348 Congress St
■ 617 737 1234 ■ $$

Barbara Lynch's funky, upscale
lunch counter serves comfort food
Italian-style, with dishes such as
Roman gnocchi, and polenta with
wild mushrooms or oxtail ragout.

7 Taranta
MAP Q2 ■ 210 Hanover St
■ 617 720 0052 ■ Closed L Sun
■ No DA ■ $$$

A creative and unusual blend of
Sardinian and Peruvian cuisine
spells intense flavors (pork with
vinegar peppers and broccoli).

8 Ristorante Fiore
MAP R1 ■ 250 Hanover St
■ 617 371 1176 ■ Closed L Sun ■ $$

Traditional southern Italian cuisine
with a strong Italian-American
accent has made this a popular
dining spot, especially with its
outdoor rooftop terrace.

9 Chart House
MAP R2 ■ 60 Long Wharf
■ 617 227 1576 ■ $$$

Housed in a historic, 18th-century
building at Long Wharf, this upscale,
waterfront restaurant offers inventive
seafood dishes. Opt for the local
catch specials.

10 Prezza
MAP R1 ■ 24 Fleet St ■ 617
227 1577 ■ Closed L, Sun ■ $$$

With one of the longest wine lists in
town, Prezza is bound to offer just
the right glass to accompany its
hearty Tuscan fare as well as its
sinfully rich desserts.

See map on p94

TOP 10 Downtown and the Financial District

Old Granary Burying Ground

The heart of Boston lies between Boston Common and the harbor. Boston has great respect for its past and there are reminders of history embedded in the center of this metropolis. The 18th-century grace of the Old State House still shines within a canyon of skyscrapers. The heroes of Boston's early years – city founder John Winthrop, patriot Paul Revere, and revolutionary Samuel Adams – are buried just steps from sidewalks abuzz with shoppers. Rolled in to this amorphous area is Faneuil Hall Marketplace, the oldest of Boston's commercial districts, and the Financial District.

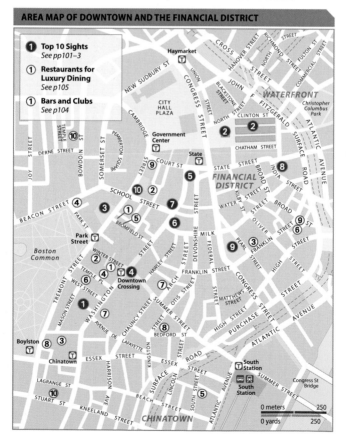

AREA MAP OF DOWNTOWN AND THE FINANCIAL DISTRICT

1 Top 10 Sights
See pp101–3

1 Restaurants for Luxury Dining
See p105

1 Bars and Clubs
See p104

Brattle Book Shop, Ladder District

1 Ladder District
MAP P4

The network of short streets linking Washington and Tremont streets has assumed a modern identity as the Ladder District. Once derelict and abandoned after dark, the area now throbs with bars, restaurants, and clubs. Anchoring the district are the ultra-chic Millennium Tower that towers over Boston Common (see pp18–19), the luxurious Ritz-Carlton, and the top-of-the-line AMC Loews cineplex (175 Tremont St). A few stalwarts, such as landmark bookseller Brattle Book Shop, are holding out against the big boys.

2 Faneuil Hall Marketplace
MAP Q2 ■ 1 Faneuil Hall Square ■ 617 523 1300 ■ Open 10am–9pm Mon–Sat, noon–6pm Sun ■ www.faneuilhallmarketplace.com

Many a fiery speech urging revolution echoed in Faneuil Hall in the late 18th century; in the 1820s it was the city's food distribution that was revolutionized in adjacent Quincy Market. Today the buildings and surrounding plazas form a shopping and dining destination – the model for dozens of markets worldwide.

3 Old Granary Burying Ground
MAP P3 ■ Tremont St at Park St ■ 617 635 4505 ■ Open 9am–5pm daily

Dating from 1660, the Granary contains the graves of many of Boston's most illustrious figures, including John Hancock, Samuel Adams, and Paul Revere (see p44), who joined his revolutionary comrades here in 1818. Other notables include the influential architect Charles Bulfinch, the parents of Benjamin Franklin, and Crispus Attucks – an escaped slave who was allegedly the first casualty of the so-dubbed Boston Massacre (see p14).

4 Downtown Crossing
MAP P4 ■ Junction of Summer, Winter & Washington Sts

This pedestrian-friendly shopping area is dominated by Macy's department store. Pushcart vendors offer more quirky goods, and food carts provide quick lunches for Downtown office workers.

5 Old State House
MAP Q3 ■ Washington & State Sts ■ 617 720 1713 ■ Open 9am–5pm daily (late May–early Sep: until 6pm) ■ Adm ■ www.revolutionaryboston.com

Built in 1713 as the seat of colonial government, the Old State House was sited to look down State Street to the shipping hub of Long Wharf. In 1770, the Boston Massacre (see p14) occurred outside its doors, and on July 18, 1776, the Declaration of Independence was first read to Bostonians from its balcony. Today, it's home to the Bostonian Society and Old State House Museum.

Old State House

Historic facade of Old South Meeting House

6 Old South Meeting House
MAP Q3 ▪ 310 Washington St ▪ 617 482 6439 ▪ Open Apr–Oct: 9.30am–5pm daily; Nov–Mar: 10am–4pm daily ▪ Adm ▪ www.oldsouthmeetinghouse.org

Old South's rafters have rung with many impassioned speeches exhorting the overthrow of the king, the abolition of slavery, women's right to vote, an end to apartheid, and many other causes. Nearly abandoned when its congregation moved to Back Bay in 1876, it was saved in one of Boston's first acts of preservation.

7 Old Corner Bookstore
MAP P3 ▪ 1 School St

This enduring spot on the Freedom Trail remains one of the most tangible sites associated with the writers of the New England Renaissance of the last half of the 19th century. Both the *Atlantic Monthly* magazine and Ticknor & Fields (publishers of Ralph Waldo Emerson and Henry David Thoreau) made this modest structure their headquarters during the mid and late 19th century, when Boston was the literary, intellectual, and publishing center of the country.

Saving the site from demolition in 1960 led to the formation of Historic Boston Incorporated. The building, however, is no longer connected to publishing today.

8 Custom House
MAP Q3 ▪ 3 McKinley Sq ▪ 617 310 6300 ▪ Tours 2pm Sat–Thu ▪ Adm

When the Custom House was built in 1840, Boston was one of America's largest overseas shipping ports, and customs fees were the mainstay of the Federal budget. The Neo-Classical structure once sat on the waterfront, but now stands two blocks inland. The 16-story Custom House tower, added in 1913, was Boston's first skyscraper. Since the 1990s, peregrine falcons have nested in the clock tower under the watchful eyes of wildlife biologists. The lobby displays a few historical artifacts, and tours of the tower give sweeping views of the harbor and city skyline.

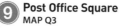

Custom House clock tower

9 Post Office Square
MAP Q3

On a sunny day this green oasis in the heart of the Financial District is filled with office workers who claim a bench or a spot of grass for a picnic. Surrounding the park are several of the area's most architecturally distinctive buildings, including the Art Deco post office building (Congress St), the Renaissance Revival former Federal Reserve building (now the Langham, Boston hotel, *see p146*), and the splendid Art Moderne New England Telephone building (185 Franklin St).

Post Office Square

10 King's Chapel
MAP P3 ■ 58 Tremont St
■ 617 523 1749 ■ Open 10am–4pm daily; recitals: 12:15pm Tue ■ Tours of crypt and bell tower: adm
■ www.kings-chapel.org

The first Anglican Church in Puritan Boston was established in 1686 to serve British Army officers. When the majority of Anglicans fled Boston along with retreating British forces in the evacuation of 1776, the chapel became the first Unitarian Church in the New World. The church is known for its program of classical concerts.

Interior of King's Chapel

A SHOPPING SPREE

▶ MORNING

The "T" will deposit you at Downtown Crossing, where you can peruse the fashions and accessories of **Macy's** at leisure. Then proceed to check out **H&M** *(350 Washington St)* for the latest in Euro styles and **DSW Shoe Warehouse** *(385 Washington St)* for a great selection of fashion shoes at discount prices. Make a left up Bromfield Street to peruse the fine writing implements and elegant stationery at **Bromfield Pen Shop** *(5 Bromfield St)*. The walk to Quincy Market down Franklin Street will take you past the Financial District with its tall and imposing skyscrapers. Turn left at Post Office Square for lunch at **Sip Café** *(Post Office Square Park)*.

AFTERNOON

Stop to enjoy a short rest outside **Quincy Market** *(see p13)* before you begin your spree in earnest. Numerous name-brand shops such as **Victoria's Secret** await. For a more local flavor try **Newbury Comics**, which carries a variety of Boston-themed gifts and paraphernalia. Then pay a visit to **Local Charm** for jewelry by local and national designers. Have an early dinner and make new friends at the communal tables at **Durgin Park** *(North Market, 617 227 2038)*. Order the gigantic prime rib and the Indian pudding (a cornmeal-molasses dish) for dessert. After dinner, rock out to live music at the **Hard Rock Café** *(22–24 Clinton St, 617 424 7625)*.

See map on p100 ←

Bars and Clubs

Beantown Pub

1 Beantown Pub
MAP P3 ▪ 100 Tremont St

This no-frills locals' hangout is filled with numerous pool tables and even more TVs, all of which are tuned to big sports games and events.

2 Mojito's
MAP P4 ▪ 48 Winter St

This vibrant Downtown Crossing nightspot has a lively, Latin music and dance scene on the weekends, and an enthusiastic international crowd.

3 Bond Lounge
MAP Q4 ▪ Langham Hotel, 250 Franklin St

Easily the most exclusive watering hole in Boston, this bar exudes old money, which is fitting for the former Governor's Reception Room of the Federal Reserve Bank.

4 Stoddard's Fine Food & Ale
MAP P4 ▪ 48 Temple Pl

Handsome, retro-themed bar in the heart of the Ladder District. Beer aficionados choose from one of the area's longest lists.

5 Silvertone Bar & Grill
MAP P3 ▪ 69 Bromfield St ▪ Closed Sun

This surprisingly unpretentious, contemporary jazz bar and casual restaurant makes an excellent place to sip good-value wine, kick back, and engage in intelligent conversation with your neighbors.

6 JM Curley
MAP G4 ▪ 21 Temple Pl

Named for Boston's old-time felonious mayor, this bar has good pub victuals (served until late) and an exhaustive list of craft and mass-market beers.

7 Central Bistro
MAP G4 ▪ 101 Arch St

A quarter of this spacious bistro is devoted to the swank, Parisian-style bar, which has great cordials, wines, and cocktails. Try the classic gin and Champagne cocktail, Soixante Quinze.

8 Good Life Downtown
MAP P4 ▪ 28 Kingston St

This retro, lounge-lizard bar and club with two dance floors gets lively after work and on weekend nights. Cocktails are top notch.

9 Times Irish Pub & Bar
MAP R3 ▪ 99 Broad St

You can usually get a table at this large pub. Settle in for a night of live music and taste some of the 20 beers on tap.

10 Jacob Wirth
MAP P5 ▪ 31 Stuart St

Dating back to 1868, Jacob Wirth retains its authentic German charm as boisterous crowds hoist large steins of fresh imported beers.

Jacob Wirth exterior

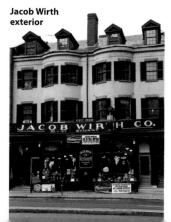

Restaurants for Luxury Dining

PRICE CATEGORIES
For a three-course meal for one with half
a bottle of wine (or equivalent meal),
taxes, and extra charges.

$ under $40 $$ $40–$60 $$$ over $60

Legal Crossing dining room

 Yvonne's
MAP G4 ■ 2 Winter Pl ■ 617
267 0047 ■ Closed L ■ $$$

A modern twist to the concept of
a supper club, Yvonne's dishes up
contemporary American fare and
a well-chosen collection of wines
and cocktails.

 Ruth's Chris Steak House
MAP P3 ■ 45 School St ■ 617 742
8401 ■ Closed L Sat & Sun ■ $$$

Classy steak emporium located in
the historic Old City Hall building.
Fine service, top-notch wine list.

3 **blu**
MAP P4 ■ 4 Avery St ■ 617 375
8550 ■ $$$

Light, fresh, delicately nuanced, and
artistically presented international
cuisine is complemented by soaring
Post-Modern architecture.

 No 9 Park
MAP P3 ■ 9 Park St ■ 617 742
9991 ■ $$$

Hobnob with Beacon Hill highflyers
in this bold bistro overlooking Boston
Common, where Mediterranean
flavors meet an imaginative wine list.

5 **O Ya**
MAP H5 ■ 9 East St ■ 617 654
9900 ■ Closed Sun & Mon ■ $$$

One of the city's priciest and fanciest
restaurants, serving modern Japanese
creations close to South Station.

6 **Umbria Prime**
MAP R3 ■ 295 Franklin St
■ 617 338 1000 ■ Closed Sun ■ $$$

Top American beef and New England
seafood are prepared with Italian
flair in the glitzy Financial District.

 Legal Crossing
MAP P3 ■ 558 Washington St
■ 617 692 8888 ■ $$$

Yet another popular offshoot of the
iconic local Legal Sea Foods empire
(see p68), serving exceptionally fresh
seafood, as always, along with cool,
Downtown-influenced cocktails.

8 **Teatro**
MAP P4 ■ 177 Tremont St
■ 617 778 6841 ■ Closed L ■ No
reservations ■ $$

A glamorous hipster scene prevails
at superchef Jamie Mammano's
theatrically styled trattoria, which
boasts a killer wine list to go with
its classic pizzas, pastas, and grills.

9 **The Oceanaire Seafood Room**
MAP Q3 ■ 40 Court St ■ 617 742
2277 ■ $$$

This former bank retains its marble
glamour in its current role as an
outstanding seafood restaurant,
with a superb raw bar and regional,
seasonal dishes on the menu.

10 **Grotto**
MAP N3 ■ 37 Bowdoin St
■ 617 227 3434 ■ $$

A nightly fixed-price menu of hearty
Italian dishes, such as sweet potato
ravioli with roasted chestnuts, makes
for luxury dining on a budget in a
brick-walled underground setting.

See map on p100

TOP 10 Chinatown, the Theater District, and South End

Boston's compact Chinatown is one of the oldest and most significant in the US, concentrating a wealth of Asian experience in a small patch of real estate. Theater-goers find the proximity of Chinatown to the Theater District a boon for pre- and post-show dining. The Theater District itself is among the liveliest in the US, and its architecturally distinctive playhouses are nearly always active, often with local productions. Adjoining the Theater District to the south is South End, once an immigrant tenement area and now Boston's most diverse neighborhood by race, cultural background,

Tremont Street town-house windows

and sexual orientation. The country's largest historical district of Victorian town houses, South End has been undergoing gentrification since the 1980s and today is home to a burgeoning, energetic club, café, and restaurant scene.

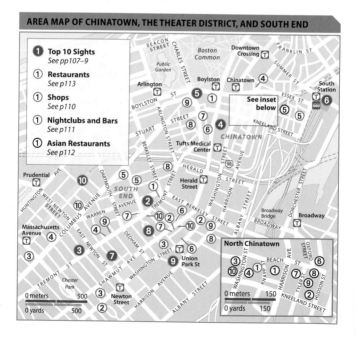

AREA MAP OF CHINATOWN, THE THEATER DISTRICT, AND SOUTH END

1 **Top 10 Sights**
See pp107–9

1 **Restaurants**
See p113

1 **Shops**
See p110

1 **Nightclubs and Bars**
See p111

1 **Asian Restaurants**
See p112

North Chinatown

0 meters 500
0 yards 500

0 meters 150
0 yards 150

Dragon Gate entrance to Chinatown on Beach Street

1 Beach Street and Chinatown

MAP P5

As the periphery of ethnic Chinatown becomes increasingly homogenized, Beach Street remains the purely Chinese heart of the neighborhood, home to the traditional apothecaries and other merchants who serve a primarily immigrant population. An ornate Dragon Gate at the base of Beach Street creates a ceremonial entrance to Chinatown. The wall behind the adjacent small park is painted with a dreamy mural of a Chinese sampan boat.

2 Boston Center for the Arts

The massive Cyclorama building is the centerpiece of the BCA, a performing and visual arts complex dedicated to nurturing new talent. The center provides studio space to about 50 artists, and its Mills Gallery mounts rotating visual arts exhibitions. The BCA's four theaters host avant-garde productions of dance, theater, and performance art *(see p60)*.

3 Tremont Street

MAP N5–M6

The part of Tremont Street between East Berkeley and Massachusetts Avenue is the social and commercial heart of the South End. Many of the handsome brick and brownstone town houses have been restored to perfection, some with a boutique or café added at street level; others remain boarded up and awaiting renovation. The liveliest corner of the South End is the intersection of Tremont with Clarendon and Union Park streets, where the Boston Center for the Arts and a plethora of restaurants and cafés create a compact entertainment and dining district.

4 Citi Performing Arts Center – Wang Theatre

With a theater modeled on the Paris Opera House and a foyer inspired by the Palace of Versailles, the opulent Wang Theatre (opened 1925) is a grand venue for touring musicals, blockbuster concerts, and local productions *(see p60)*.

Grand foyer of Wang Theater

5 Piano Row
MAP N4

In the late 19th century, the head-quarters of leading piano makers Steinert, Vose, Starck, Mason & Hamlin, and Wurlitzer were all located on the section of Boylston Street facing Boston Common, giving the block (now a historic district) its nickname of Piano Row. Over a century later, those Beaux Arts buildings still echo with music. The ornate Colonial Theatre is undergoing extensive renovation, which is expected to continue until 2017. Another attraction on Piano Row is Boylston Place, a small-scale club and nightlife center.

6 South Station
MAP Q5

A brick temple to mass transport-ation, the Neo-Classical Revival South Station was erected in 1898 at the height of rail travel in the US, and was once the country's busiest train station. Following extensive restoration in 1989, it now serves as an Amtrak terminal for trains from the south and west of the city, as well as a "T" stop and a social and commercial center with a lively food court and occasional free lunchtime concerts.

7 Villa Victoria
MAP F6 ▪ Area bounded by Shawmut Ave, Tremont St, W Newton St, & W Brookline St ▪ Center for the Arts: 85 W Newton St ▪ 617 927 1707 ▪ www.ibaboston.org

Villa Victoria is a virtually self-contained, primarily Hispanic neighborhood that grew out of a unique collaboration among Puerto Rican community activists, flexible city planners, and visionary archi-tects. With its low-rise buildings, narrow streets, and mom-and-pop stores, Villa Victoria replicates the feel of Puerto Rican community life. At its heart, the Center for the Arts sponsors classes and exhibitions. In mid-July the center puts on the Latino arts and cultural celebration Festival Betances.

8 Union Park
MAP F6

Constructed between 1857 and 1859, this small park surrounded by English-style brick row houses was built to contrast with the French-inspired grid layout of nearby Back Bay. Graced with lovely trees and fountains and verdant with a thick mat of grass, the square was one of the first areas in the South End to be gentrified.

South Station's imposing Neo-Classical facade

Holy Cross Cathedral

9 Holy Cross Cathedral
MAP F6 ■ 1400 Washington St
■ 617 542 5682 ■ Open 9am–3pm
daily

Holy Cross, the largest Roman
Catholic church in Massachusetts,
acts as the seat of the archbishop
of Boston. The cathedral was constructed between 1866 and 1875 (on
the site of the municipal gallows)
to serve the largely Irish-American
workers who lived in the adjoining
shantytown. Today the congregation
is principally of Hispanic origin. Of
note are the magnificent stained-
glass windows, which include rare
colored glass imported from Munich
in the 19th century, and the powerful
Hook & Hastings organ which, when
played with the stops out, seems to
make every piece of Roxbury pudding-
stone in the building reverberate.

10 Southwest Corridor Park
MAP E6

The first section of the 5-mile (8-km)
Southwest Corridor Park divides
South End and Back Bay along
the "T" orange line corridor. In the
residential South End portion, a path
strings together numerous small
parks. Between Massachusetts
Avenue and West Roxbury, the park
broadens to include amenities such
as tennis and basketball courts.

EXPLORING CHINATOWN AND SOUTH END

▶ MORNING

Begin on **Washington Street**
where you can peruse the exotic
produce, Chinese teas, imported
Asian spices, and specialty foods
at **Jia Ho** *(see p110)*. Continue
down Essex Street, ducking into
Oxford Place to see the mural,
Travelers in an Autumn Landscape,
based on the scroll painting by
the same name at the Museum
of Fine Arts. The distinctive and
colorful **Dragon Gate** to Chinatown
stands at the corner of Edinboro
Street and Beach Street, along
with pagoda-style phone booths.
Continue on to Chauncy Street
and peruse colorful fabrics and
materials at **Winmil Fabrics** *(see
p110)*. Then stop for a delicious
lunch at **Shabu-Zen** *(see p112)*.

AFTERNOON

Walk down Tremont Street to the
South End, or hop on the "T" two
stops to Back Bay Station. Head
west on Columbus Avenue to see
the elaborate bronze sculptures
that tell the story of escaped
slave Harriet Tubman, who led
many others to freedom on the
Underground Railroad, a series of
hiding places in non-slave states.
Back at Tremont Street, visit the
Boston Center for the Arts *(see
p107)* to get a snapshot of local
contemporary art at the Mills
Gallery. Then, if you have time,
stroll around gracious **Union Park**
before returning to the arts center
for dinner and live music at **The
Beehive** *(see p62)*. There is a good
chance that local jazz artists will
be playing.

See map on p106 ←

Shops

1 Jia Ho Supermarket
MAP N5 ▪ 692 Washington St

This compact market offers vegetables, tropical fruits, and packaged foods essential for cuisines from Singapore to Seoul.

2 Flock

MAP P6 ▪ 274 Shawmut Ave
▪ Closed Mon

Flock sells stylish and easy-to-wear women's clothing and accessories with a modern Bohemian flair, plus an eclectic range of gifts and afford-able home decor items.

3 Hudson

MAP F6 ▪ 12 Union Park St

This home decor boutique by interior designer Jill Goldberg offers home furnishings and a delightfully eclectic mix of decorative accent pieces that includes traditional, country, vintage, and modern pieces.

4 Winmil Fabrics
MAP P5 ▪ 111 Chauncy St

This popular, family-owned shop offers a great selection of fabrics, buttons, and patterns, all at great prices.

5 Tadpole
MAP M6 ▪ 58 Clarendon St

If there was ever any doubt that young families are colonizing the South End, then Tadpole's cheery selection of clothing, toys, and accessories for children dispels it.

Tadpole on Clarendon Street

Lekker Home linens

6 Lekker Home
MAP G6 ▪ 1313 Washington St
▪ Closed Mon

Contemporary Italian, Scandinavian, and German home design items are the highlights of this emporium, which offers the latest trends in homeware.

7 Michele Mercaldo Jewelry
MAP G6 ▪ 276 Shawmut Ave
▪ Closed Sun

Jewelry by contemporary designer Michele Mercaldo and her colleagues is displayed in creative and unusual ways at this South End store.

8 Bead & Fiber
MAP G6 ▪ 460 Harrison Ave
▪ Closed Mon

Whether you're looking for beaded jewelry or fiber art, or simply the materials to make them, this shop and gallery offers everything you need, including classes.

9 okw
MAP F6 ▪ 631A Tremont St
▪ Closed Sun

Fashion designer Waheeda Ali-Salaam brings 21st-century pizzazz to classic women's clothing and accessories. Look for the ever-popular "interview suits."

10 Syrian Grocery Importing Company
MAP G5 ▪ 270 Shawmut Ave
▪ Closed Mon

Harking back to the South End's days as a Middle Eastern immigrant neighborhood, this grocery sells southern and eastern Mediterranean essentials, from preserved lemons to rare Moroccan argan oil.

Nightclubs and Bars

1 Whisky Saigon
MAP N5 ▪ 116 Boylston St ▪ 617 482 7799 ▪ Closed Sun–Tue ▪ Adm

The colorful and sophisticated bar up front becomes a glamorous dance scene in the back.

2 Toro
MAP F6 ▪ 1704 Washington St

Barcelona-style tapas complement an all-Spanish wine list and a select group of creative cocktails with names like Verdad y Amor (Truth and Love).

3 Wally's Café

MAP E6 ▪ 427 Massachusetts Ave

Exhale before you squeeze in the door at Wally's. This thin, chock-full sliver of a room is one of the best jazz bars in Boston, and has been since 1944.

Spanish paella at Toro

4 Five Horses Tavern
MAP F6 ▪ 535 Columbus Ave ▪ 617 936 3930

This atmospheric, brick-walled tavern boasts an impressive collection of craft beers from around the world. It also serves fine whiskeys and American comfort food.

5 Delux Café
MAP M6 ▪ 100 Chandler St ▪ Closed Sun

Cheap drinks and an Elvis shrine lend an edge to the trendy scene here. It's good clean fun for hipster grandchildren of the beatniks. Regulars and visitors alike rave about the grilled cheese.

6 Royale
MAP P5 ▪ 279 Tremont St ▪ 617 338 7699 ▪ Adm

This massive two-story dance hall occasionally morphs into a live-performance concert venue for touring acts.

7 Venu
MAP N5 ▪ 100 Warrenton St ▪ Closed Mon & Wed

Music varies each night of the week, but it's always the same Prada-Armani-Versace-clad crowd. The Art Deco bar makes for a beautiful look.

8 Jacque's Cabaret
MAP N5 ▪ 79 Broadway ▪ Adm

This multifaceted pioneer drag-queen bar features female impersonators, edgy rock bands, and cabaret shows.

9 J.J. Foley's Café
MAP G5 ▪ 117 E Berkeley St

This friendly club is a favorite among locals in need of a pint of beer.

10 The Butcher Shop
MAP F6 ▪ 552 Tremont St

A full-service butcher shop and wine bar pairs house-made sausages, salami, and foie gras terrine with Old World wines of Italy, France, and Spain by the glass or bottle. Gourmet "Burgers and Beers" evenings take place in the summer months.

The Butcher Shop

See map on p106 ←

Asian Restaurants

1 East Ocean City
MAP P5 ▪ 27 Beach St ▪ 617 542 2504 ▪ No DA ▪ $

Select your fish from the tanks near the front and ask the chef to recommend a dish.

2 New Shanghai
MAP H5 ▪ 21 Hudson St ▪ 617 338 0732 ▪ $

Typical southern Chinese fare is available, but best bets are lusty northern dishes like duck tea-smoked in a wok, spicy Sichuan whole fish, and Mongolian beef.

Exterior of Penang

3 Penang
MAP N5 ▪ 685 Washington St ▪ 617 451 6372 ▪ $

Nominally "pan-Asian," Penang has a chiefly Malay menu, ranging from inexpensive noodle staples to more contemporary concoctions.

4 Emperor's Garden
MAP P5 ▪ 690 Washington St ▪ 617 482 8898 ▪ $

Dim sum in this historical opera house is a theatrical experience. Note that most southern Chinese dishes are large and best shared.

5 Hei La Moon
MAP Q5 ▪ 88 Beach St ▪ 617 338 8813 ▪ $

Huge, rather formal pan-Chinese restaurant on the Leather District side of Atlantic Avenue. On weekend mornings, a large crowd is guaranteed for the dim sum.

6 Taiwan Cafe
MAP P5 ▪ 34 Oxford St ▪ 617 426 8181 ▪ No credit cards ▪ No DA ▪ $

The typically Taiwanese over-bright cafeteria appearance should not deter aficionados of authentic, adventurous dishes like spicy pig ears and jellyfish.

7 Shojo
MAP P5 ▪ 9A Tyler St ▪ 617 423 7888 ▪ $$

Savor suckling pig *bao* (steamed stuffed bun) and chicken tacos with *yuzu* slaw at this snazzy Japanese restaurant. Superb craft cocktails.

8 China King
MAP P5 ▪ 60 Beach St ▪ 617 542 1763 ▪ $

This eatery offers an extensive menu of Chinese delicacies, plus the must-try Peking duck. Order it a day ahead for a minimum of four diners.

9 Shabu-Zen
MAP P5 ▪ 16 Tyler St ▪ 617 292 8828 ▪ No DA ▪ $

Choose your meats and vegetables and your cooking liquid, then swish away to nirvana.

10 Dumpling Café
MAP G5 ▪ 695 Washington St ▪ 617 338 8858 ▪ $

This casual spot sells several varieties of dumpling made fresh daily, alongside delicacies such as dishes using duck tongue.

Diners at Dumpling Café

Restaurants

PRICE CATEGORIES

For a three-course meal for one with half a bottle of wine (or equivalent meal), taxes, and extra charges.

....

$ under $40 $$ $40–$60 $$$ over $60

1 Picco
MAP F5 ▪ 513 Tremont St ▪ 617 927 0066 ▪ $

This friendly little place is popular for its thin-crust, wood-fired pizzas and decadent homemade ice cream.

2 Myers + Chang
MAP G6 ▪ 1145 Washington St ▪ 617 542 5200 ▪ $$

Clever reinventions of classic Chinese dishes, such as lemon shrimp dumplings; also vegetarian-friendly. Sake-based cocktails with guava and lychee are a big hit.

3 El Centro
MAP F6 ▪ 472 Shawmut Ave ▪ 617 262 5708 ▪ $

Authentic Mexican cuisine from a Sonoran chef emphasizes fresh flavors and serves authentic tamales and tortillas made from scratch.

4 Tremont 647
MAP F6 ▪ 647 Tremont St ▪ 617 266 4600 ▪ Closed L Mon–Sat ▪ $$

Chef Andy Husbands' New American cooking favors big portions, bold flavors, and lots of wood-grill smoke with the superb-quality meat.

5 Les Zygomates
MAP Q5 ▪ 129 South St ▪ 617 541 5108 ▪ Closed Sun ▪ $$$

French bistro fare, dozens of wines by the glass, and live jazz is on offer near Boston South Station.

6 Coppa
MAP F6 ▪ 252 Shawmut Ave ▪ 617 391 0902 ▪ Closed L Sat ▪ $

Small, Italian-inspired plates make Coppa perfect for grazing while sipping glasses of wine and basking in the romantic ambience.

Aquitaine's classically French interior

7 Aquitaine
MAP F5 ▪ 569 Tremont St ▪ 617 424 8577 ▪ Closed L Mon–Fri ▪ $$$

A Parisian-style bistro popular for its snazzy wine bar and its French market-style cooking. Black truffle vinaigrette makes Aquitaine's steak-frites Boston's best.

8 Masa
MAP N6 ▪ 439 Tremont St ▪ 617 338 8884 ▪ Closed L ▪ $$

Refined New American dishes with southwestern accents are complemented by killer margaritas, colorful decor, and good wines.

9 Ostra
MAP N5 ▪ 1 Charles St S ▪ 617 421 1200 ▪ $$$

This sophisticated restaurant in the Theater District serves contemporary Mediterranean fare in both innovative and classic preparations.

10 Giacomo's
MAP L6 ▪ 431 Columbus Ave ▪ 617 536 5723 ▪ $

This offshoot of a very popular North End eatery offers heaped portions of filling Italian fare at great prices. The restaurant accepts cash only.

See map on p106 ←

🔟 Kenmore and the Fenway

On days when the Red Sox are playing a home baseball game at Fenway Park, Kenmore Square is packed with fans. By night, Kenmore becomes the jump-off point for a night of dancing, drinking, and socializing at clubs on or near Lansdowne Street. Yet for all of Kenmore's genial rowdiness, it is also the gateway into the sedate parkland of the Back Bay Fens and the stately late 19th- and early 20th-century buildings along the Fenway. The Fenway neighborhood extends all the way southeast to

Huntington Avenue, aka the "Avenue of the Arts," which links key cultural centers such as Symphony Hall, Huntington Theatre, the Museum of Fine Arts, Massachusetts College of Art and Design, and the delightful and not-to-be-missed Isabella Stewart Gardner Museum along a tree-lined boulevard.

Entrance to the Back Bay Fens

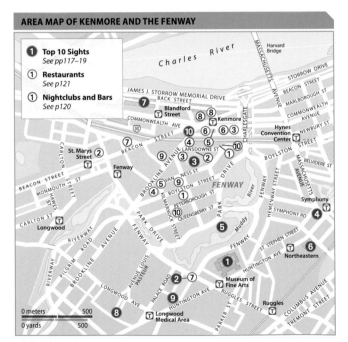

AREA MAP OF KENMORE AND THE FENWAY

① **Top 10 Sights**
See pp117–19

① **Restaurants**
See p121

① **Nightclubs and Bars**
See p120

1 Museum of Fine Arts

One of the most comprehensive fine arts museums in the country, the MFA is especially renowned for its collections of French Impressionism and of ancient Egyptian and Nubian art and artifacts. Its Asian art holdings are said to be the largest in the United States (see pp28–31).

2 Isabella Stewart Gardner Museum

This Fenway museum, in a faux Venetian palace, represents the exquisite personal tastes of its founder, Isabella Stewart Gardner, who was one of the country's premier art collectors at the end of the 19th century (see pp34–5).

3 Fenway Park

MAP D5 ■ 4 Yawkey Way ■ 617 267 1700 for tickets, 617 226 6666 for tours ■ Tours year-round: 9am–5pm daily (to 4pm in winter; last tour 4 hours before game time) ■ Adm ■ www.redsox.com

Built in 1912, the home field of the Boston Red Sox is the oldest surviving park in major league baseball, and aficionados insist that it's also the finest. An odd-shaped parcel of land gives the park quirky features, such as the high, green-painted wall in left field, affectionately known as "the Green Monster." Although previous owners threatened to abandon Fenway, the current ones have enlarged the park to accommodate more loyal Sox fans. Behind-the-scenes tours include areas normally closed to the public, like the dugouts and private boxes.

Symphony Hall

4 Symphony Hall

The restrained, elegant Italian Renaissance exterior of this 1900 concert hall barely hints at what is considered to be the acoustic perfection of the interior hall, as designed by Harvard physics professor Walter Clement Sabine. Home of the Boston Symphony Orchestra, the hall's 2,361 seats are usually sold out for their classical concerts, as well as for the lighter Boston Pops (see p60).

5 Back Bay Fens

MAP D5–D6 ■ Bounded by Park Dr & The Fenway

This lush ribbon of grassland, marshes, and stream banks follows Muddy River and forms one link in the Emerald Necklace of parks (see p19). The enclosed James P. Kelleher Rose Garden in the center of the Fens offers a perfect spot for quiet contemplation. A path runs from Kenmore Square to the museums and galleries on Huntington Avenue, which makes a pleasant shortcut through the Fens.

Fenway Park baseball park

Magnificent interior of Jordan Hall

6 Jordan Hall

This 1,013-seat concert hall at the New England Conservatory of Music opened in 1903 and underwent an $8.2 million restoration in 1995. Musicians often praise its acoustics, heralding Jordan as "the Stradivarius of concert halls." Hundreds of free classical concerts are performed at this National Historic Landmark hall every year (see p61).

Photographic Resource Center

7 Boston University

MAP C4 ■ Howard Gotlieb Archival Research Center: 771 Commonwealth Ave ■ 617 353 3696 ■ Exhibit rooms open 9am–4pm Mon–Fri
MAP C5 ■ Photographic Resource Center: 832 Commonwealth Ave ■ 617 975 0600 ■ Open Sep–Jun ■ Call for timings and off-season schedule ■ Adm ■ www.bu.edu

Founded as a Methodist Seminary in 1839, Boston University was chartered as a university in 1869. Today it enrolls approximately 30,000 students from all 50 states and some 125 countries. The scattered colleges and schools were consolidated at the Charles River Campus in 1966. Both sides of Commonwealth Avenue are lined with distinctive university buildings and sculptures. The Howard Gotlieb Archival Research Center is big on the memorabilia of show business figures, displayed on a rotating basis. Artifacts include Gene Kelly's Oscar and a number of Bette Davis's film scripts. It also exhibits selections from its holdings of rare manuscripts and books. The Photographic Resource Center, a focus for Boston's considerable photographic community, frequently mounts challenging exhibitions of local and international photographers, as well as students of local colleges.

8 Warren Anatomical Museum

MAP C6 ■ 10 Shattuck St ■ 617 432 6196 ■ Open 9am–5pm Mon–Fri

Established in 1847 from the private holdings of Dr. John Collins Warren, this museum contains the former anatomical teaching collections of the Harvard Medical School, including clinical examples of rare deformities and diseases. Among the displays are several delicate and poignant skeletons of stillborn conjoined twins. The collections are still used for medical education.

9 Massachusetts College of Art and Design Galleries

MAP D6 ▪ 621 Huntington Ave ▪ 617 879 7333 ▪ Open noon–6pm Mon–Sat (to 8pm Wed) ▪ www. massart.edu

The Paine and Bakalar galleries in the South Building of the Massachusetts College of Art and Design mount some of Boston's most dynamic exhibitions of contemporary visual art. It is the only independent state-supported art college in the US and exhibitions tend to emphasize avant-garde experimentation as well as social commentary and documentary.

10 Kenmore Square

MAP D5

Largely dominated by Boston University, Kenmore Square is now being transformed from a student ghetto into an extension of upmarket Back Bay, losing some of its funky character but gaining élan in the process. As the public transportation gateway to Fenway Park, the square swarms with baseball fans and sidewalk vendors, rather than students, on game days. The most prominent landmark of the square is the CITGO sign, its more than 9,000 ft (2,743 m) of LEDs pulsing red, white, and blue from dusk until midnight. *Time* magazine designated this sign an "objet d'heart" because it was so beloved by Bostonians that they prevented its dismantling in 1983.

Kenmore Square, with its CITGO sign

A DAY OF THE ARTS

> ### MORNING AND AFTERNOON

Take the green line "T" (B train) to Boston University Central and make your way to the **Howard Gotlieb Archival Research Center**, part of Boston University, for a glimpse of Fred Astaire's dancing shoes and other show business ephemera. Then head west toward **Kenmore Square** to explore the stores, including the encyclopedic Boston University Bookstore (660 Beacon St), directly under the CITGO sign. Stroll along Brookline Avenue to **Fenway Park** for a tour of the stadium *(see p117)* and then take Yawkey Way to the **Back Bay Fens** *(see p117*, where you can rest beneath the wings of the angel on the Veteran's Memorial. Continue to the **Museum of Fine Arts** *(see pp28–31)* to view the outstanding art collections – from ancient Egyptian artifacts to contemporary installations. Afterward, follow the Fenway three blocks left to continue your immersion in art at the **Isabella Stewart Gardner Museum** *(see pp34–5)*. Take a break in the "living room" of the museum's Renzo Piano-designed wing, then grab a bite to eat at the classy **Café G** *(see p121)*.

> ### EVENING

You can pack in a full evening of entertainment by taking in a recital at **Jordan Hall** *(see p61)*. When the final applause has died down, make your way to **Jillian's** entertainment complex *(see p120)* and round off the night with billiards, bowling, and dancing that could go on into the very early hours.

See map on p116 ←

Nightclubs and Bars

 Loretta's Last Call
MAP D5 ■ 1 Lansdowne St
Country music and Southern food fuel this happening bar and dance club. The interior has a cozy, vintage ambience.

 Bleacher Bar
MAP D5 ■ 82A Lansdowne St
Tiny bar tucked in the back of Fenway Park, with several seats offering direct views into the historic venue. Inviting pub fare and a well-stocked bar keep customers occupied.

 Game On!
MAP D5 ■ 82 Lansdowne St
Wall-to-wall TVs are tuned to every game that's on anywhere in the country at this bar in a corner of Fenway Park. A prime spot for sports fans to eat, drink, and cheer.

 Cask 'n Flagon
MAP D5 ■ 62 Brookline Ave
■ Closed Sun
At Fenway's premier sports bar, fans hoist a cold one and debate the merits of the Sox manager's latest tactics.

 Hawthorne
MAP D5 ■ Hotel Commonwealth, 500 Commonwealth Ave
Cocktails and champagnes star in this upscale lounge for Kenmore Square adults who would rather converse than yell.

Elegant Hawthorne lounge–bar

Game On! sports bar

 Lower Depths Tap Room
MAP D5 ■ 476 Commonwealth Ave
This underground bar in Kenmore Square features tater tots and beer cheese dip on the menu, plus an extensive list of local craft brews. There are good options for retro drinkers, such as the Genesse Cream Ale. The bar accepts cash only.

 Audubon Boston
MAP D5 ■ 836 Beacon St
Close enough to Fenway Park to drop by after the game, Audubon Boston is a relaxed neighborhood bar and grill with good food, beer, and a thoughtful wine list.

 Cornwall's Pub
MAP D5 ■ 654 Beacon St
Offering the very best of both worlds, Cornwall's is a British-style pub with a wide range of good beers, ales, and food, but the bartenders also understand baseball.

 Boston Beer Works
MAP D5 ■ 61 Brookline Ave
This cavernous brew pub specializes in lighter American ales and serves giant plates of ribs and chicken that can easily feed two ravenous Red Sox fans.

 Jillian's
MAP D5 ■ 145 Ipswich St
Set behind Fenway Park, this entertainment complex features a choice of bars, bowling lanes, and pool tables, as well as the popular dance club, Tequila Rain.

Restaurants

1 Citizen Public House
MAP E5 ▪ 1310 Boylston St
▪ 617 450 9000 ▪ $

Craft beers, 100 whiskeys, excellent cocktails, and great pub food make Citizen a top neighborhood spot.

2 Elephant Walk
MAP C5 ▪ 900 Beacon St
▪ 617 247 1500 ▪ Closed L Sat & Sun
▪ $$

This welcoming local institution has remained in popular demand for years for its Cambodian-French fare served in an airy bamboo-trimmed dining room.

3 Joséphine
MAP D4 ▪ 468 Commonwealth Ave ▪ 617 375 0699 ▪ $$$

A Parisian-style restaurant, Joséphine adds a contemporary touch to classic French dishes such as foie gras, pan-seared scallops, and veal cheeks. The lemon tart is delicious.

Sweet Cheeks

4 Sweet Cheeks
MAP E5 ▪ 1381 Boylston St
▪ 617 266 1300 ▪ $

Chef-owner Tiffani Faison is crazy about authentic Southern barbecue. Order pork belly by the pound and drink sweet tea from Mason jars.

PRICE CATEGORIES

For a three-course meal for one with half a bottle of wine (or equivalent meal), taxes and extra charges.

$ under $40 $$ $40–$60 $$$ over $60

---

5 Wahlburgers
MAP D5 ▪ 132 Brookline Ave
▪ 617 927 6810 ▪ $

Chef Paul, brother of actor Mark Walhberg, runs this tongue-in-cheek joint that serves burgers with a twist.

6 Eastern Standard
MAP D5 ▪ 528 Commonwealth Ave ▪ 617 532 9100 ▪ $$$

Buttoned-down versions of continental classics have some hidden surprises on this menu, such as magnificent salt-cod fritters and Boston cream pie.

7 Café G
MAP D6 ▪ 280 Fenway ▪ 617 566 1088 ▪ Closed D, Mon ▪ $

Superb light fare, rich desserts, and fine wines complete a visit to the Isabella Stewart Gardner Museum *(see pp34–5)*.

8 UBurger
MAP D5 ▪ 636 Beacon St
▪ 617 536 0448 ▪ $

What a concept – fast food, but made to order, and just as you like it. With over two dozen toppings you can truly customize your burger.

9 Tasty Burger
MAP D5 ▪ 1301 Boylston St
▪ 617 425 4444 ▪ $

This no-frills burger joint in the shadow of Fenway Park offers a variety of toppings and a wide assortment of beer.

10 El Pelon Taqueria
MAP D5 ▪ 92 Peterborough St
▪ 617 262 9090 ▪ $

A charming little eatery that churns out tasty authentic Mexican treats at very competitive prices.

See map on p116

TOP 10 Cambridge and Somerville

Harvard may be Cambridge's undeniable claim to worldwide fame, but that is not to diminish the city's vibrant neighborhoods, superb restaurants, unique shops, and colorful bars lying just beyond the school's gates. Harvard Square, with its international newsstands, name-brand shopping, and numerous coffeehouses, is a heady mix of urban bohemia and Main Street USA. To the northwest, the heavily residential city of Somerville is distinguished by its tightly knit European-style squares, where tourists seldom tread and local character abounds.

Peabody Museum exhibit

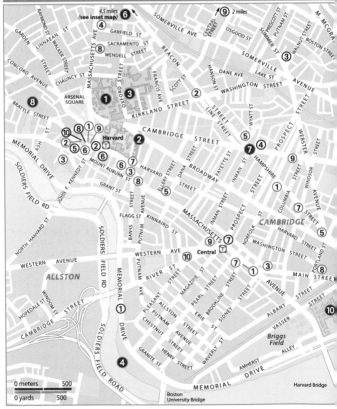

AREA MAP OF CAMBRIDGE AND SOMERVILLE

1 Harvard University

While its stellar reputation might suggest visions of ivory towers in the sky, Harvard is a surprisingly accessible, welcoming place. Still, too often, visitors limit themselves to what is visible from the Yard: Massachusetts Hall, the Widener Library, maybe University Hall. But with other buildings by Gropius and Le Corbusier, top-notch museums, the eclectic Harvard Square, and performing arts spaces such as the Loeb Drama Center and Memorial Hall's Sanders Theatre *(see p61)* lying just beyond the university, Harvard provides every incentive to linger a while *(see pp20–23)*.

2 Harvard Art Museums

MAP B1 ■ **32 Quincy St** ■ **617 495 9400** ■ **Open 10am–5pm daily** ■ **Adm** ■ **www.harvard artmuseums.org**

Harvard has some of the world's finest collegiate art collections. The Fogg, Sackler, and Busch-Reisinger museums, which make up the Harvard Art Museums, share space in an Renzo Piano-designed facility. Visitors will enjoy the surprising juxta-positions of Chinese bronzes, Greek vases, medieval altarpieces, and German Expressionist paintings with a visit to all three *(see pp20–23)*.

Natural History Museum

3 Peabody and Natural History Museums

MAP B1 ■ **Peabody Museum: 11 Divinity Ave** ■ **617 496 1027** ■ **Open 9am–5pm daily** ■ **Adm**
MAP B1 ■ **Natural History Museum: 26 Oxford St** ■ **617 495 3045** ■ **Open 9am–5pm daily** ■ **Adm** ■ **www. peabody.harvard.edu, http://hmnh. harvard.edu**

Its ongoing commitment to research aside, the Peabody Museum excels at illustrating how interactions between distinct cultures have affected peoples' lives and livelihoods. Its North American Indian exhibit displays artifacts that reflect the aftermath of encounters between white Europeans and Native Americans. The Natural History museum delves even deeper in time, exhibiting eons-old natural wonders *(see pp20–21)*.

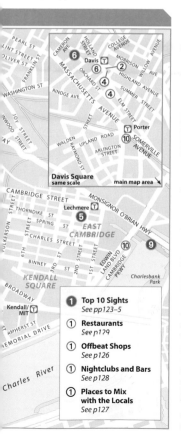

Davis Square
same scale   main map area ↘

1 **Top 10 Sights**
See pp123–5

① **Restaurants**
See p129

① **Offbeat Shops**
See p126

① **Nightclubs and Bars**
See p128

① **Places to Mix with the Locals**
See p127

4 Charles Riverbanks
MAP B2–F3

Whether you're cheering the rowers of the Head of the Charles Regatta (see p77) or watching the "T" cross Longfellow Bridge through a barrage of snowflakes, the banks of the Charles River offer a fantastic vantage point for taking in Boston's celebrated scenes. On summer Sundays, the adjacent Memorial Drive becomes a sea of strollers, joggers, and rollerbladers (see p127).

5 Cambridge Multicultural Arts Center
MAP F2 ■ 41 2nd St ■ 617 577 1400 ■ Open 10:30am–6pm Mon–Fri

Housed in a beautiful 19th-century courthouse, the CMAC presents a range of performance and visual art exhibitions which promote cross-cultural exchange, including summer concerts in Kendall Square. A unique feature is the encouragement of dialogue between audience and artist after performances and openings.

Cambridge Multicultural Arts Center

Somerville Theatre, Davis Square

6 Davis Square
With its cooler-than-thou coffee shops, lively bar scene, affordable restaurants, and the renowned Somerville Theatre (see p60), Davis Square, Somerville, stands as the area's most desirable neighborhood for many young Bostonians. And with prestigious Tufts University a 10-minute walk away, the square's youthful spirit is in a constant state of replenishment.

7 Inman Square
MAP D1

Oft-overlooked Inman Square is possibly Cambridge's best-kept secret. Home to such renowned restaurants and cafés as the East Coast Grill and 1369 (see p127), ace jazz club Ryles (see p63), plus Christina's delectable ice creams (see p71), Inman handsomely rewards those who are willing to go out of their way to experience a real-deal Cambridge neighborhood.

8 Longfellow House
MAP A1 ■ 105 Brattle St ■ 617 876 4491 ■ Open Jun–Oct: tours 10:30am–4pm Wed–Sun ■ www.nps.gov/long

Poet Henry Wadsworth Longfellow can be credited with helping to shape Boston's – and America's – collective identity. His poetic documentation of Paul Revere's midnight ride (see p44) immortalized both him and his subject. In 1837, Longfellow took up residence in this house, a few blocks from Harvard Yard. He was not the house's first illustrious resident. General George Washington headquartered and planned the 1776

LOCAL STAGES

The performing arts form part of the character of Cambridge and Somerville. The ornate Somerville Theatre (see p60) draws nationally recognized musical acts, while the Loeb Drama Center (64 Brattle Street, 617.547.8300) stages The American Repertory Theatre's daring, top-notch productions. And Harvard student-produced pieces grace the Hasty Pudding Theatre's stage (12 Holyoke St, Cambridge, 617 495 5205).

siege of Boston in these rooms. The building is preserved with furnishings of Longfellow's and Washington's time, and houses the poet's archives.

9 Museum of Science

MAP N1 ■ Science Park ■ 617 723 2500 ■ Open 9am–5pm Mon–Thu, Sat & Sun (Jul–Sep: to 7pm), 9am–9pm Fri ■ Adm ■ www.mos.org

Exploring the cosmos in the Hayden Planetarium, hitting the high notes on a musical staircase, experiencing larger-than-life IMAX films in the Mugar Omni Theater – the Museum of Science certainly knows how to make learning enjoyable. In addition to these attractions, the museum hosts blockbuster shows like Harry Potter: The Exhibit. Live presentations take place throughout the day.

Massachusetts Institute of Technology

10 Massachusetts Institute of Technology (MIT)

MAP D3 ■ 77 Massachusetts Ave ■ 617 253 4795 ■ List Visual Arts Center: 20 Ames St, Cambridge ■ 617 253 4680 ■ Open noon–6pm Tue–Sun (to 8pm Thu) ■ MIT Museum: 265 Massachusetts Ave ■ 617 253 5927 ■ Open 10am–5pm daily ■ Adm ■ www.mit.edu

MIT has been the country's leading technical university since its founding in 1861. Its List Visual Arts Center exhibits work that comments on technology or employs it in fresh, surprising ways. Also of note is the MIT Museum, with its interactive exhibits on such fascinating topics as artificial intelligence, holography, and the world's first computers.

THE CAMBRIDGE CURRICULUM

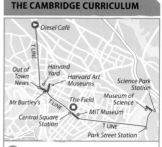

▶ MORNING

Begin your morning with a cup of gourmet coffee and light break-fast at the popular **Diesel Café** on Davis Square. Next, ride the "T" inbound to Harvard and head straight to **Out of Town News** (0 Harvard Sq) to peruse the mind-boggling selection of international newspapers and magazines. Visit **Harvard Yard** (see p20) and the John Harvard Statue and then walk east to Quincy Avenue and north to the **Harvard Art Museums** (see p123). Walk south to Massachusetts Avenue, and turn right to legendary **Mr Bartley's** (1246 Massachusetts Ave) for a lunch of speciality burgers and sweet potato fries.

AFTERNOON

Ride the "T" inbound to Central Square, and walk southeast along Massachusetts Avenue to the **MIT Museum**, where interactive exhibits of scientific, artistic and technological innovations reflect the creative energy of MIT. Return to Central Square and ride the "T" to Park Street. Then ride the Green Line "T" to Science Park and the **Museum of Science**. In this amazing museum you can choose from 700 interactive exhibits, hop aboard a simulator and take an orbital journey around the International Space Station, watch cosmic collisions, and explore the biology of human life. Then retrace your route on the "T" to Central Square, where you can sit back and enjoy a refreshing glass of Guinness in the convivial atmosphere at **The Field** (120 Prospect St).

See map on pp122–3 ←

Offbeat Shops

1 Black Ink
MAP B1 ▪ 15 Brattle St, Cambridge

From aluminum ring binders to spring-clip photo frames, Black Ink features quirky items you didn't know you couldn't live without.

2 Magpie
416 Highland Ave, Somerville

Packed with handmade crafts, art by local artists, and goods from indie designers, this hipster Davis Square boutique playfully advertises "shiny things for your nest."

3 Revolution Books
MAP B2 ▪ 1158 Massachusetts Ave, Cambridge ▪ Closed Sun & Mon

Che Guevara and Mao Tse-Tung are alive and well here. You can read up on Communism and purchase left-leaning T-shirts, posters, and buttons.

4 Abodeon
1731 Massachusetts Ave, Cambridge

Abodeon stocks home furnishings of the decidedly retro variety. Items include 1940s rolling chaise longues, vintage cocktail services, and even the occasional Wurlitzer jukebox.

5 Hubba Hubba
MAP C2 ▪ 2 Ellery St, Cambridge ▪ Closed Sun

If Cambridge's Puritanical founders could see it... fetishist accessories, spiked belts, sexy leather corsets, and not-so-innocent toys line the shelves of this risqué boutique.

6 The Million Year Picnic
MAP A1 ▪ 299 Mt Auburn St, Cambridge

New England's oldest comic bookstore keeps its faithful customers happy with an extensive back-issue selection, graphic novels, rare imports, and all the latest indie comics, along with toys and T-shirts.

7 Oona's Experienced Clothing
MAP B2 ▪ 1210 Massachusetts Ave, Cambridge

This secondhand store has been stocking vintage as well as modern clothes since 1972.

Bags of seeds from Magpie

8 Games People Play
MAP B1 ▪ 1100 Massachusetts Ave, Cambridge

Board games, card games, role-playing games, word games, action games, puzzles... if someone plays it, Games People Play either sells it or can order it in for you in a couple of days.

9 Cardullo's Gourmet Shoppe
MAP B1 ▪ 6 Brattle St, Cambridge

Harvard Square's oldest culinary store specializes in gourmet foods and beverages from around the world. You can also buy made-to-order deli sandwiches for lunch.

Cardullo's Gourmet Shoppe

10 Porter Exchange Mall
1815 Massachusetts Ave, Cambridge

Take a trip to Asia in this renovated 1928 Art Deco building, housing a Japanese-style noodle hall and gift shops with all sorts of wonderful Far Eastern ephemera.

See map on pp122–3

Places to Mix with the Locals

Memorial Drive in the fall

1 Memorial Drive
MAP B4–F3

Memorial Drive is a magnet for joggers and rollerbladers. On summer Sundays, the road closes to vehicular traffic and becomes the city's best people-watching spot.

2 The Pit
MAP B1 ■ Bounded by JFK St & Massachusetts Ave, Cambridge

On and around this sunken brick platform, street musicians, protesters, punk rockers, and uncategorizables create a scene worthy of a *Life* magazine spread.

3 The Neighborhood
MAP D1 ■ 25 Bow St, Somerville ■ 617 623 9710 ■ $

Sunday brunch at the Neighborhood brings throngs intent on securing seating beneath the outdoor grape arbors. Equally coveted are the Portuguese breakfast bread platters.

4 1369 Coffee House
MAP D1 ■ 1369 Cambridge St, Cambridge ■ 617 576 1369 ■ $

Set on Inman Square, this branch of 1369 has poetry readings, mellow music, and courteous staff, which give it a neighborly atmosphere.

5 Brattle Theatre
MAP B1 ■ 40 Brattle St, Cambridge ■ 617 876 6837

A Harvard Square institution, the Brattle screens cinema greats daily. Rainy afternoon? Take in a 2-for-1 Fellini double feature for under $15.

6 Au Bon Pain
MAP B1 ■ 1360 Massachusetts Ave, Cambridge ■ 617 497 9797 ■ $

Every kind of Cambridge character can be found sipping coffee and munching croissants on the plaza at Holyoke Center. Top amusement? Challenging the chess masters to a speed game.

7 Improv Boston
MAP C2 ■ 40 Prospect St, Cambridge ■ 617 576 1253

The improvisational comedy troupe here will often explore the offbeat side of Boston life and welcomes audience participation.

8 Club Passim
MAP B1 ■ 47 Palmer St, Cambridge ■ 617 492 7679

The subterranean epicenter of New England's thriving folk music scene regularly welcomes nationally renowned artists. It also has an inventive vegetarian kitchen, Veggie Planet.

9 Trum Ball Fields
Broadway, Somerville

Summer in Somerville is epitomized by one thing: baseball at the playground. On most weeknights, you can watch energetic youngsters take their swings.

10 Dado Tea
MAP B1 ■ 50 Church St, Cambridge ■ 617 547 0950

This Harvard Square hangout, owned by locals, is a serene, tranquil place to settle in with a cup of exotic tea and healthy pastries, sandwiches, wraps, and salads.

For a key to restaurant price ranges see p129

Nightclubs and Bars

The Middle East music club

1 The Middle East
MAP D3 ▪ 472–480 Massachusetts Ave, Cambridge ▪ 617 864 3278 ▪ Adm

A live music club to rival any in New York or Los Angeles, the Middle East rocks its patrons from three stages and nourishes them with delicious kebabs and curries.

2 Sinclair
MAP B1 ▪ 52 Church St

Harvard Square's primary live gig venue attracts a wide assortment of acts. The front room doubles as a trendy restaurant and lounge, and it's open into the small hours every night of the week.

3 Regattabar
MAP B2 ▪ 1 Bennett St, Cambridge ▪ Closed Sun & Mon

Befitting its location in the sleek Charles Hotel, Regattabar offers a refined yet casual setting for watching jazz giants. Shows sell out quickly.

4 The Burren
247 Elm St, Somerville ▪ 617 776 6896

This friendly Irish bar features live music almost every night, and the performances range from Irish sessions to bluegrass to swing and jazz. The backroom has comedy, step-dancing, and a weekly open mic.

5 Trina's Starlite Lounge
MAP D1 ▪ 3 Beacon St, Somerville

A relaxed vibe, cheap beer, and diner-style food like chicken, waffles, and Sloppy Joes makes Trina's the preferred hangout for a generation of Somerville-Cambridge hipsters.

6 Hong Kong
MAP B2 ▪ 1238 Massachusetts Ave, Cambridge ▪ Comedy club closed Sun

Chinese food at ground level gives way to a bustling lounge on the second floor and a raucous comedy nightclub on the third. Tuesday night features a comic magic show.

7 Lord Hobo
MAP D ▪ 292 Hampshire St, Cambridge

Forty draft beers, homey bistro food, and an inventive cocktail program attract an eclectic crowd, from hipsters to software geeks.

8 Lizard Lounge
MAP B1 ▪ 1667 Massachusetts Ave, Cambridge

Just outside Harvard Square, the Lizard Lounge attracts a young, alternative rock- and folk-loving crowd with the promise of good live music and a small cover charge.

9 The Cantab Lounge
MAP C2 ▪ 738 Massachusetts Ave, Cambridge

Live local rock performances, poetry slams, open mic nights, and other such events light up the small but lively stage at this blue-collar beer bar in Central Square.

10 River Gods
MAP C3 ▪ 125 River St, Cambridge

Eccentric decor, video game nights, and a hip crowd make this one of Boston's more interesting nightspots. The nightly entertainment switches between DJs and live acts.

Restaurants

PRICE CATEGORIES

For a three-course meal for one with half a bottle of wine (or equivalent meal), taxes, and extra charges.

$ under $40 $$ $40–$60 $$$ over $60

1 Oleana
MAP D2 ▪ 134 Hampshire St, Cambridge ▪ 617 661 0505 ▪ Closed L daily ▪ $$$

Chef Ana Sortun's mastery of spices is evident in Oleana's sumptuous Middle Eastern cuisine, served in a casually elegant dining room and a pretty courtyard with a fountain.

2 The Kirkland Tap & Trotter
MAP C1 ▪ 425 Washington St ▪ 857 259 6585 ▪ $$$

Chef Tony Maws of Craigie on Main fame showcases his simpler, yet creative, home-style dishes in casual environs. Try the unique cocktails.

The Kirkland Tap & Trotter

3 Craigie On Main
MAP D3 ▪ 853 Main St, Cambridge ▪ 617 497 5511 ▪ $$$

"Nose-to-tail" fine dining is the style at Tony Maw's main venue. The menu changes daily, and includes six- and eight-course tasting versions.

4 Posto
MAP B2 ▪ 187 Elm St, Somerville ▪ 617 625 0600 ▪ Closed L Mon–Sat ▪ $

Handmade pastas, Naples-certified pizza, and wood-grilled meats and fish make Posto one of the most popular restaurants in Davis Square.

5 Atasca
MAP D2 ▪ 50 Hampshire St, Cambridge ▪ 617 621 6991 ▪ $$

The bold flavors of Portugal are yours for the tasting at the warmly appointed, cozy Atasca. Flavorful sautés and rustic grilled dishes are just some of its many charms.

6 Redbones
55 Chester St, Somerville ▪ 617 628 2200 ▪ $

Redbones' kitchen creates some of the best barbecue north of the Carolinas, and the atmosphere is emphatically Southern.

7 Viale
MAP C3 ▪ 502 Massachusetts Ave, Cambridge ▪ 617 576 1900 ▪ Closed L daily ▪ $$$

Delightful Mediterranean dishes – many available as small plates – and innovative cocktails make this friendly bar-restaurant a go-to place for food and drinks.

8 Area 4
MAP D2 ▪ 500 Technology Sq, Cambridge ▪ 617 758 4444 ▪ $

Food is served as early as 7am at this bakery-café, and continues into the night with New American comfort food and pizzas.

9 Puritan & Company
MAP D2 ▪ 1166 Cambridge St, Cambridge ▪ 617 876 0286 ▪ Closed L Mon–Sat ▪ $$$

Excellent farm-to-table dining venue that re-invents New England cuisine with dishes such as seared scallops with tomatillos. Sunday brunch is a major foodie scene.

10 Restaurant Dante
MAP F3 ▪ 40 Edwin H. Land Blvd, Cambridge ▪ 617 497 4200 ▪ $$$

Creative interpretations of contemporary Italian cuisine are the highlights of this riverside room at the Royal Sonesta (see p147).

See map on pp122–3 →

🔟 South of Boston

South of Fort Point Channel, Boston's neighborhoods of Jamaica Plain, Roxbury, Dorchester, and South Boston are a mixture of densely residential streets and leafy parklands that form part of Frederick Law Olmsted's Emerald Necklace *(see p19)*. The lively street scenes of Boston's African-American, Latin-American, and Irish-American communities make the city's southerly neighborhoods a dynamic ethnic contrast to the more homogenized city core. Often ignored by tourists, the area south of Boston is full of quirky shops, local bars, hot nightclubs, and great off-beat places to enjoy ethnic food. This area is a little harder to reach but it is worth the effort to experience a more edgy, diverse Boston.

Forest Hills Cemetery

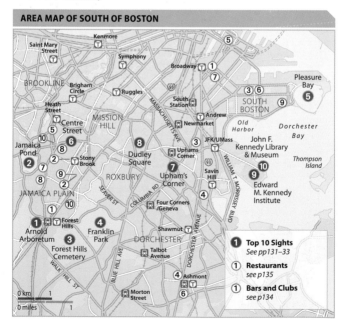

AREA MAP OF SOUTH OF BOSTON

① **Top 10 Sights**
See pp131–33

① **Restaurants**
see p135

① **Bars and Clubs**
see p134

1 Arnold Arboretum
125 Arborway, Jamaica Plain
617 524 1718

One of the US's foremost collections of temperate-zone trees and shrubs covers the peaceful 0.4-sq mile- (1.1-sq km-) arboretum. Grouped in scientific fashion, they are a favorite subject for landscape painters, and a popular resource for botanists and gardeners. The world's most extensive lilac collection blooms from early May through late June, and thousands of Bostonians turn out for Lilac Sunday, in mid-May, to picnic and enjoy the peak of the Syringa blooms. The main flowering period of mountain laurel, azaleas, and other rhododendrons begins around Memorial Day (at the end of May).

Arnold Arboretum

within the city. Locals take avidly to the 1.5-mile (2.5-km) bankside path or fish in the 53-ft- (16-m-) deep glacial kettle pond (fishing requires a Massachusetts license – call 617 626 1590). The boathouse rents small sailboats, kayaks, and rowboats in summer.

2 Jamaica Pond
Jamaica Pond Boathouse, Jamaica Way 617 522 5061
Open mid-Apr–Oct: noon–sunset Mon, Wed, & Thu (from 10am Fri–Sun) www.cityofboston.gov/parks

This appealing large pond and its surrounding leafy park was landscaped by Frederick Law Olmsted to accentuate its natural glacial features and it offers an enchanting piece of countryside

Forest Hills Cemetery

3 Forest Hills Cemetery
95 Forest Hills Ave, Jamaica Plain 617 524 0128

More than 100,000 graves dot the rolling landscape in this Victorian "garden cemetery," one of the first of its kind. Maps available at the entrance identify the graves of notable figures, such as poet e e cummings and playwright Eugene O'Neill. Striking memorials include the bas-relief *Death Stays the Hand of the Artist* by Daniel Chester French, near the main entrance.

4 Franklin Park
Franklin Park Rd, Dorchester 617 265 4084

Frederick Law Olmsted considered Franklin Park the masterpiece of his Emerald Necklace *(see p19)*, but his vision of urban wilds has since been modified to more modern uses. The park is home to the second-oldest municipal golf course in the US and the child-friendly Franklin Park Zoo *(see p51)*, which contrasts contemporary ecological exhibits with charming zoo architecture, such as a 1913 Oriental bird house.

Jamaica Pond

Sandy beach at tranquil Pleasure Bay

5 Pleasure Bay

South Boston's Pleasure Bay park encloses a pond-like cove of Boston Harbor with a causeway boardwalk, where locals turn out for their daily constitutionals. Castle Island, now attached to the mainland, has guarded the mouth of Boston Harbor since the first fortress was erected in 1634. As New England's oldest continually fortified site, it's now guarded by Fort Independence (c. 1851). Anglers gather on the adjacent Steel Pier and drop bait into the midst of striped bass and bluefish runs.

6 Centre Street

Jamaica Plain is home to many artists, musicians, and writers as well as a substantial contingent of Boston's gay and lesbian community. Centre Street is the main artery and hub. There is a distinctly Latin-American flavor at the Jackson Square end, where Caribbean music shops and Cuban, Dominican, and Mexican

Centre Street

eateries abound. At the 600 block, Centre Street morphs into an urban counter-cultural village, with design boutiques, funky second hand stores, and small cafés and restaurants.

7 Upham's Corner

Strand Theatre, 543 Columbia Rd, Dorchester ▪ 617 635 1403
The area known as Upham's Corner was founded in 1630, and its venerable Old Dorchester Burial Ground contains ethereal carved stones from this Puritan era. Today, Upham's Corner is decidedly more Caribbean than Puritan, with shops specializing in food, clothing, and the music of the islands. The Strand Theatre, a 1918 luxury movie palace and vaudeville hall, functions as an arts center and venue for live concerts and religious revival meetings.

8 Dudley Square

Hamill Gallery of Tribal Art, 2164 Washington St, Roxbury ▪ 617 442 8204 ▪ Open noon–6pm Thu–Sat Dillaway-Thomas House, 183 Roxbury St, Roxbury ▪ 617 445 3399 ▪ Call in advance for tour hours
Roxbury's Dudley Square is the heart of African-American Boston as well as the busiest hub in Boston's public transportation network. The Beaux Arts station is modeled on the great train stations of Europe. Among the square's many shops and galleries is the Hamill Gallery of Tribal Art, as much a small museum as a gallery. A few blocks from the square, the modest Georgian-style

Dillaway-Thomas House reveals Roxbury's early history, including the period when it served as HQ for the Continental Army's General John Thomas during the Siege of Boston.

⑨ Edward M. Kennedy Institute for the United States Senate

210 Morrissey Blvd, Dorchester ■ **617 740 7000** ■ **Open 9am–5pm Tue–Sat, 10am–5pm Sun** ■ **Adm** ■ **www.emkinstitute.org**

Displaying re-creations of the US Senate Chamber and Senator Edward M. Kennedy's office, this facility provides an impressive interactive experience of how the Senate functions. The 'People Who Made a Difference' exhibit highlights citizens who made an impact on civic life.

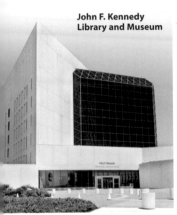

John F. Kennedy Library and Museum

⑩ John F. Kennedy Library and Museum

Columbia Point, Dorchester ■ **617 514 1600** ■ **Open 9am–5pm daily** ■ **Adm** ■ **www.jfklibrary.org**

This nine-story pyramidal building designed by I. M. Pei in 1977 stands like a billowing sail on Columbia Point. Inside, exhibits recount the 1,000 days of the Kennedy presidency. Kennedy was the first president to grasp the power of broadcast, and video exhibits include campaign debates, as well as coverage of his assassination and funeral.

STREET HEAT & POND COOL IN JAMAICA PLAIN

▶ AFTERNOON

The Orange Line "T" delivers you to the Latin end of Jamaica Plain's **Centre Street** at Jackson Square, where life is more Santo Domingo than downtown Boston. Head west and ease into the rhythm by sampling empanadas, coffee, and Latin desserts at **Gondres Bakery** *(333 Centre St)*. A walk along Centre Street serves up a cornucopia of Latino fashion and specialty shops. **Del Valle's Children's Gift Shop** *(360 Centre St)* has clothing, from christening gowns and rompers to dress shoes and jewelry. Follow Centre Street as it doglegs left. Hip **Streetcar** *(488 Centre Street)* carries a large selection of boutique wines and craft beers. At **J P Licks** *(659 Centre St)* order a cone of super-premium ice cream, and continue to **Boing! JP's Toy Shop** *(667 Centre St)* to discover fun gifts for kids from one to 91. Jeweler Phil Celeste carries unique clothing, jewelry and gift items at **On Centre** *(676 Centre St)*, while **Fire Opal** *(683 Centre St)* showcases handmade American art, apparel, and jewelry. The thrift store **Boomerangs** *(716 Centre St)* has clothing and home decor. Stroll up Burroughs Street and cross Jamaicaway to **Jamaica Pond** *(see p131)* to stroll, sit in the shade, or rent a rowboat.

EVENING

Once you've worked up an appetite, return to Centre Street for dinner at **Vee Vee** *(see p135)*. Afterward, hit ultra-hip **Milky Way Lounge** *(see p134)* for a chilled beer, live music, and dancing.

See map on p130 ←

Bars and Clubs

 The Jeannie Johnston
144 South St, Jamaica Plain

This entertainment venue has plenty to offer, with an open mic on Thursdays, live local bands on Fridays, and karaoke on Saturdays, as well as a snug spot to sit with one of its 27 draught or bottled beers.

 Milky Way Lounge
284 Amory St, Jamaica Plain

Situated in JP's legendary Brewery Complex, Latinos and Jamaica Plain hipsters rub shoulders at the Milky Way. They come for the dancing, the latest local live bands, and the exceptional cosmopolitans.

 Playwright Bar
658 East Broadway, South Boston

A spiffy Dublin-style pub with good food, excellent pints, and large windows that let in the sunlight and the breeze.

 Dbar
1236 Dorchester Ave, Dorchester

The eclectic dinner menu disappears around 10pm, when Dbar morphs into a hopping, diverse nightclub where brightly colored cocktails are a specialty. Show tunes on Tuesdays, rock videos on Fridays.

 Lucky's Lounge
355 Congress St, South Boston

A Fort Point Channel underground bar that swaggers with rat pack retro ambience, right down to the lounge acts and the unmissable Frank Sinatra tribute nights.

 Boston Beer Garden
734 East Broadway, South Boston

On weekends this watering hole is packed both inside and outside in the garden. Modern pub food hits a fairly high mark.

 Amrheins
80 West Broadway, South Boston

The vintage bar at Amrheins – a South Boston fixture since 1890 – is reason enough to visit the 'hood. Locals debate the issue of the day over a drink or two.

8 **Brendan Behan Pub**
378 Centre St, Jamaica Plain

This Irish pub is frequented by neighborhood types with vaguely poetic pretensions, and outfitted with Guinness and Murphy's on tap. Live music most nights.

9 **Local 149**
149 P St, South Boston

This South Boston neighborhood joint features 22 beers on tap, plus innumerable cans and bottles, and some of the best New American food outside of a fancy restaurant.

 Doyle's Café
3484 Washington St, Jamaica Plain

The apex of Irish-American political culture, Doyle's has been serving beer since 1882, and corned beef and cabbage on Thursdays for as long as anyone can remember. Busy nightly.

Doyle's Café

Restaurants

PRICE CATEGORIES

For a three-course meal for one with half a bottle of wine (or equivalent meal), taxes, and extra charges.

$ under $40 $$ $40–$60 $$$ over $60

1 Coppersmith
40 W 3rd St, South Boston ■ 617 658 3452 ■ Closed Mon and L Tue–Fri ■ $$

This vast converted warehouse has an American bistro restaurant as well as two food trucks serving global fare. Try the BBQ popcorn.

Tres Gatos

2 Tres Gatos
470 Centre St, Jamaica Plain ■ 617 477 4851 ■ $

This combination tapas bar and book/music store features authentic Spanish bar dishes along with some inventive variants.

3 224 Boston Street
224 Boston St, Dorchester ■ 617 265 1217 ■ Closed L ■ $

This chef-driven northern Italian trattoria is the longest lasting and most successful restaurant in the 'hood. Enjoy a Tuscan feast for half the price of North End's restaurants.

4 Ashmont Grill
MAP D4 ■ 555 Talbot Ave, Dorchester ■ 617 825 4300 ■ Open daily for D and L Mon–Fri, brunch Sat & Sun ■ $$

Veteran chef Chris Douglass uses local produce to conjure up contemporary bistro delights.

5 El Miami Restaurant
381 Centre St, Jamaica Plain ■ 617 522 4644 ■ $

This place is the self-proclaimed "King of the Cuban sandwiches." Check out the photos of the Latino pro baseball players who often eat here when in town.

6 Tavolo
1918 Dorchester Ave, Dorchester ■ 617 822 1918 ■ Closed L ■ $

Superb, rustic Italian cuisine emphasizes fresh market dining in this Ashmont neighborhood.

7 Ten Tables
597 Centre St, Jamaica Plain ■ 617 524 8810 ■ Closed L ■ $

This small venue has just ten tables with, an equally compact but rewarding menu, such as scallops on minted pea tendrils.

8 Vee Vee
763 Centre St, Jamaica Plain ■ 617 522 0145 ■ Closed L and Mon ■ $$

Delectable American bistro fare makes this 35-seat restaurant a favorite with local foodies, especially since many dishes have vegetarian versions. The Sunday brunch is very popular.

9 Bella Luna
280 Armory St, Jamaica Plain ■ 617 524 6060 ■ $$

The dining room adjacent to the Milky Way Lounge, Bella Luna shoots the moon with bright salads, rib-sticking Italian fare such as chicken marsala, and their signature gourmet pizzas.

10 Blue Nile
389 Centre St, Jamaica Plain ■ 617 522 6453 ■ Closed Mon ■ $

Ethiopian home-style food celebrates fresh vegetables as well as meats and fish, and there's plenty of choice for vegans as well. *Teff injera*, the sourdough pancakes that double as utensils, are made on the premises.

See map on p130

Boston Streetsmart

Boston street signs

Getting To and Around Boston

Arriving by Air

Logan International Airport (BOS) lies 2 miles (3 km) northeast of Downtown. Over 30 international, domestic, and international airlines serve the Boston area.

Transportation to central Boston is accessed from the baggage claim area. Taxis wait at all terminals but airport fees can make a downtown trip expensive ($20–$30). The cheapest way to get into town is by the **MBTA** Silver Line bus service (approx. 15 mins). Free buses link terminals to the subway. Shuttle services are available via **Massport** to Downtown Boston and Cambridge hotels, and to locations throughout Massachusetts.

The most scenic route is by water – take an airport shuttle bus to Logan Dock. The **City Water Taxi** crosses the harbor to Atlantic Avenue; **Boston Harbor Water Taxi** runs to 14 destinations in summer; and the **Rowes Wharf Water Taxi** serves Rowes Wharf and Boston Harbor Hotel.

Some domestic and several international charter flights use **Manchester Airport (MHT)**, New Hampshire, 50 miles (79 km) from Boston, and **TF Green Airport (PVD)**, near Providence, Rhode Island, 59 miles (95 km) from Boston. Buses to Boston run from both.

Arriving by Train

Amtrak intercity rail transportation arrives into Boston at South Station (Atlantic and Summer Sts) via Back Bay station (145 Dartmouth St). New York City services are frequent and take between three and five hours.

Arriving by Car

Most major northeast highways converge on Boston, with I-95 (also known as Route 128) bypassing the city center. I-90, the Massachusetts Turnpike, comes in from the west. I-93 crosses the city north to south as an underground expressway, known as the Thomas P. 'Tip' O'Neill Jr. Tunnel. Watch signs carefully for exits. The purple-lit Zakim suspension bridge, connecting underground and surface highways, provides a northern gateway to Boston.

Arriving by Bus

The primary bus station, South Station Transportation Center (700 Atlantic Ave,) is used by a dozen bus companies providing intercity service, as well as Amtrak and the MBTA subway system. **Greyhound Lines** connect with over 3,700 locations, and offer low-cost passes. Other lines include **Bolt Bus**, **Megabus**, and **Peter Pan**.

Arriving by Ship

Cruise ships dock at Black Falcon Terminal, South Boston, which is a $10 taxi ride to Downtown. On Port of Call days, the local trolley tour companies *(see p144)* offer services to popular destinations.

Traveling by Public Transportation

The subway and trolley system (the "T"), buses, commuter rail and ferries are run by the **Massachusetts Bay Transportation Authority (MBTA)**.

The MBTA subway and trolley system gets you close to almost anywhere in the city *(see back flap for "T" map)*. Fares are $2.65 almost everywhere, and buying a reuseable, rechargeable CharlieCard reduces the fare to $2.10.

The MBTA bus system enlarges the transit network to cover more than 1,000 miles (1,620 km). Buses run less frequently than the "T." Make sure you have exact change ($2.10) or a CharlieCard when traveling by bus. Bus maps are available on the MBTA website or at the main office at Downtown Crossing. The Silver Line is technically a "T" line but actually runs buses, and provides quick trips to airport or cruise ship terminals.

A LinkPass for unlimited MBTA travel, including inner harbor ferries, can be purchased on a CharlieCard for $12 (one day) and $19 (seven days) at most subway stations.

Traveling by Car

Driving is the least efficient way to get around Downtown Boston, and can be stressful. Locals drive quite aggressively, and the narrow streets are congested and laid out in a confusing manner with little signage. There are few gas stations, limited parking with time-of-day restrictions, one-way streets and traffic circles. For those drivers who are not familiar with the city, an up-to-date GPS system and advance planning are essential.

Parking in a lot is very expensive, costing about $35 per day or about $12 for one hour in the Boston Common Garage in the city center. Other parking lots in the area charge more. On-street parking meters have a two-hour maximum, residents-only rules are strictly enforced, and fines are high.

Most car rental companies have desks at Logan Airport. Drivers must be aged between 21 and 75 with a valid license. All agencies require a credit card or cash deposit. Collision damage waiver and liability insurances are recommended.

Traveling by Water Taxi and Ferry

City Water Taxi operates throughout Boston's inner harbor. **Boston Harbor Cruises** offers ferries to Salem and Provincetown from Long Wharf. The **Bay State Cruise Company** connects the World Trade Center with Provincetown, and the inexpensive MBTA Harbor Express Long Wharf to Charlestown Navy Yard.

Traveling by Taxi

Taxis can be hired on the street in the Downtown area or at taxi stands. You can also call to arrange a pick up. **Uber** and **Lyft** let you summon a ride-share car by smartphone, billing your credit card.

Walking and Cycling

Downtown Boston is compact and easy to get around on foot. It has many bike paths including on some major streets. Cycling on highways is illegal and riding on sidewalks is discouraged or illegal. **Hubway** has bike sharing at 140 stations throughout the city.

DIRECTORY

AIRPORTS

Logan International Airport
[617 561 1800
w massport.com

Manchester Airport
[603 624 6556
w flymanchester.com

TF Green Airport
[401 737 8222
w pvdairport.com

AIRPORT TRANSFERS

Massport
w massport.com

Star Shuttle
[617 230 6005
w starshuttleboston.com

TRAIN

Amtrak
[800 872 7245
w amtrak.com

BUS LINES

BoltBus
[877 265 8287
w boltbus.com

Greyhound Lines, Inc.
[800 231 2222
w greyhound.com

Megabus
[877 462 6342
w megabus.com

Peter Pan Bus Lines
[401 751 8800
w peterpanbus.com

PUBLIC TRANSPORTATION

MBTA
[617 222 3200
w mbta.com

TAXIS

Boston Cab
[617 536 5010

Independent Taxi Operators Association
[617 825 4000

Metro Cab Association
[617 782 5500

Yellow Cab Cambridge
[617 547 3000

WATER TAXIS

Bay State Cruise Company
[617 748 1428
w baystatecruise company.com

Boston Harbor Cruises
[617 227 4321
w bostonharborcruises. com

Boston Harbor Water Taxi
[617 593 9168
w bostonharborwatertaxi. com

City Water Taxi
[617 422 0392
w citywatertaxi.com

MBTA Harbor Express
[617 222 6999
w mbta.com

Rowes Wharf Water Taxi
[617 406 8584
w roweswharfwater transport.com

RIDESHARE, CARSHARE, BIKESHARE COMPANIES

Hubway
w thehubway.com

Lyft
w www.lyft.com

Uber
w uber.com

Practical Information

Passports and Visas

Canadian and Mexican visitors require valid passports to enter the US. Citizens of 38 countries, including most European nations, Australia and New Zealand, do not need a visa, but must have a passport and apply to enter in advance via the **Electronic System for Travel Authorization (ESTA)**. All other visitors require a tourist visa and passport to enter, and will be photographed and have fingerprints checked. A return airline ticket is required. Regulations may change, so check well in advance of travel with the US Department of State for the latest information.

Customs and Immigration Regulations

Nonresident travelers need to complete a **Customs and Border Protection Agency** form. Passengers may carry $100 in gifts; one liter of alcohol as beer, wine or liquor (age 21 years or older); and one carton of cigarettes, 50 cigars (not Cuban) or two kilograms (4.4 lbs) smoking tobacco without incurring tax.

Travel Safety

Visitors can get up-to-date travel safety information from the **Foreign and Commonwealth Office** in the UK, the **State Department** in the US, and the **Department of Foreign Affairs and Trade** in Australia.

Travel Insurance

Medical insurance is highly recommended for international travelers, as costs for health and dental care can be very high. Insurance against trip cancellation, air travel delays, and lost baggage is advisable. Car rental agencies offer vehicle and liability insurance, but check your policy anyway.

Health

No vaccinations are required for visiting the US. For ease of moving through airport security, pack medications in their original, labeled containers. Unused syringes are allowed along with injectable prescription medication. Your hotel will usually recommend a doctor if you require medical assistance. Hospitals offer emergency and urgent walk-in care, and minor injury clinics are available throughout the city. Some pharmacies have nurse practitioners available.

Personal Security

Boston is a large, cosmopolitan city and is usually safe in the tourist areas. However, be alert to your surroundings, leave your valuables and passport in a hotel safe, avoid obvious jewelry or displaying expensive cameras or smartphones. Keep your wallet in an inside pocket, and carry a cross-body purse. Keep copies of documents and ID, and split cash and credit cards between wallets and pockets. Keep your hotel room locked, and get a receipt for stored luggage.

If you will be out in the late evening, ask your hotel concierge for advice related to your specific destination. The likelihood of stolen property being recovered is slim, but you should file a claim with the **Boston Police Department** and retain a copy for your insurance company. Note the taxi company, bus line or metro route you use to help retrieve lost belongings. If you misplace your passport, contact your embassy straight away. Call your credit card company or bank at once to report lost or stolen cards or traveler's checks.

Currency and Banking

The US currency is the dollar ($), and the dollar is made up of 100 cents. The most common bills come in denominations of $1, $5, $10 and $20, with larger denominations available. Cents come in one (penny), five (nickel), ten (dime) and 25 (quarter) cent coins. It is advised to convert a small amount of currency at the airport to cover immediate expenses and then wait to change larger amounts at a bank or ATM using a debit card for a more favorable exchange rate. Currency bureaux such as **Travelex** can be found at Logan Airport and many other locations.

A major credit card will be needed for car rentals, hotels, and restaurants. Most services accept Visa,

Mastercard, and American Express. Cash is usually required by street vendors and on buses.

Driving License

Visitors with valid licenses from most countries can drive a vehicle while in the US, but it is advisable to bring an International Driving Permit (IDP), especially if the license is not in English, does not have a photo, or is not from a qualifying country.

Communications

Phone numbers in the US are ten digits long. The first three digits are the area code, which is 617 or 857 for Boston (including Cambridge, Brookline, and Somerville). The area codes for the region around Boston are 339 and 781. Dial the area code first, followed by the seven digit phone number. Dial 0 for the operator, and 411 for directory assistance (fee). To make a direct overseas call, dial 011, country code, city area code and number. For an operator assisted call, dial 01, country code, city area code and number.

Public telephones are rare, while making calls from your hotel room will be expensive. If you plan to use a cell phone, check with your provider about service in the US before you travel. **Cellhire,**

Cellular Abroad and others rent phones for overseas and US calls, or you can buy a disposable phone at many outlets.

Most hotels offer free Wi-Fi, but some hotels charge for this service. Free Wi-Fi is available in many public places.

Many hotels sell stamps and will mail your letters, or flat rate envelopes and boxes are available at post offices for domestic and overseas destinations.

The daily newspapers are the *Boston Globe* and *Boston Herald*. The free weekly *DigBoston* has arts and entertainment listings and the monthly *Boston Magazine* has restaurant reviews (see p144).

DIRECTORY

CUSTOMS AND VISAS

Customs and Border Protection
Visa Waiver Program, Customs information
w cbp.gov/travel

Electronic System for Travel Authorization (ESTA)
w esta.cbp.dhs.gov/esta

Transportation Security Administration
w tsa.gov/travel

TRAVEL SAFETY

Australia
w dfat.gov.au/smarttraveller.gov.au

United Kingdom
w www.gov.uk/foreign-travel-advice

United States
w travel.state.gov

EMBASSIES

British Consulate
MAP E3 ▪ One Broadway, Cambridge
w gov.uk/government/world/usa

Canadian Consulate
MAP M6 ▪ 3 Copley Place, Suite 400
w boston.gc.ca

Irish Consulate
MAP M5 ▪ 535 Boylston St, 5th Floor
w dfa.ie/irish-consulate/boston

EMERGENCY SERVICES

Medical, Ambulance, Police, Fire
(911

Boston Police Department Non-Emergency
(617 343 4200

MBTA Transit Police
(617 222 1100

PHARMACY

CVS 24-hour pharmacy
MAP L5 ▪ 587 Boylston St
(617 437 8414
MAP B1 ▪ 6 JFK St, Cambridge
(617 354 4420

WALK-IN CLINICS

CVS (minor injuries)
36 White St, Cambridge
(866 389 2727

The Doc Is In
MAP F5 ▪ 581 Boylston St Suite 800
(617 247 1400

HOSPITALS

Beth Israel Deaconess Medical Center
(617 667 7000

Boston Medical Center
(617 638 8000

Massachusetts General Hospital
(617 726 2000
Walk-In Unit
(617 726 2707

Tufts Medical Center
(617 636 5000

CURRENCY

Travelex
Logan International Airport
(617 569 6268
w travelex.com

COMMUNICATIONS

Cellhire
w cellhire.com

Cellular Abroad
w cellularabroad.com

US Postal Service
(800 275 8777
w usps.com

Time Difference

Boston is on Eastern Standard Time (EST), three hours ahead of California and five hours behind the UK. Daylight Saving Time starts at 2am on the second Sunday in March and ends on the first Sunday in November.

Electrical Appliances

The standard US electric current is 110 volts, and 60 Hz current. An adapter will be required for all European appliances.

Opening Hours

Business office hours are usually 9am–5pm. Stores open at 10am or 11am and close at 6pm to 7pm Mon–Sat. Some stores remain open later, usually on Thursday evening and during the tourist season, while on Sunday hours are usually noon–6pm. Malls are generally open Mon–Sat from 9am or 10am to 8pm or 9pm, and noon–6pm Sun. Most banks are open 9am–4pm or 5pm Mon–Fri, and some also open on Saturday morning. Grocery stores generally open 8am–9pm daily, or longer. Pharmacy hours vary, from 8am–6pm or later, and some are open 24 hours. Most museums are open 10am (noon on Sun) to 5pm, but check each listing or website before making your plans. MBTA subway trains begin at about 5am Mon–Sat, 6am on Sun, and end just after midnight Sun–Thu and about 1am or 2am Fri and Sat. Each line, and each station, varies so check ahead of travel.

Sources of Information

The Greater Boston Convention & Visitors Center gives information on their website and by phone. The site has a search function for hotels, shops, dining, sights, and transportation. Walk-in visitor information is available at the **Boston Common Visitor Center**, and at an information booth in the center court of the Prudential Center.

Boston National Historical Park Visitor Center at Faneuil Hall has visitor information about the Freedom Trail and other National Parks.

Cambridge Office of Tourism offers a Visitor Guide, an informative interactive website and phone support. Walk-in support is provided at the main office and at the Visitor Information Booth in Harvard Square.

Disabled Travelers

All facilities built or reno-vated since 1987 are legally required to provide wheel-chair accessible entrances and restrooms. Govern-ment buildings, museums, and theaters are acces-sible, but call ahead to verify that tours can meet your requirements. It is always advisable to call historic buildings, hotels, B&Bs and restaurants ahead of time to ask about specific amenities available. The Greater Boston Convention & Visitors Center website has listings that give basic accessibility information and contact numbers for a wide range of sights, venues and tours.

Guide dogs are permitted in all establishments, and most busy road inter-sections have audio signals for safe crossing times.

Most MBTA buses, sub-ways, commuter rail lines and ferries accommodate wheelchairs. MBTA also has a paratransit service for eligible patrons who cannot use the standard services. See the MBTA website for specifics. **Boston Cab** taxi company *(see p139)* will send a wheelchair accessible vehicle on request. **Logan International Airport** has accessible restrooms, ele-vators and ramps into the terminal as well as a list of accessible transportation to and from the airport on its website *(see p139)*.

Fenway Park *(see p117)* has accessible elevators, accessible spaces for wheelchair users, seats for the hearing or visually impaired, and Listening Devices can be hired.

Weather

Boston has a four season climate. Summers are warm, sometimes hot (over 81°F/27°C) and humid, and you will need sunglasses, sun hat, and sunscreen. Have a variety of clothing as the weather can be changeable with rainy, cold or windy days. Winter weather can be very cold (21°F/-6°C in January) with snow, ice and wind, and may change throughout the day. Spring and fall weather is generally pleasant, with warm days and cooler mornings and evenings. Be prepared for sun or rain, and wear comfortable walking shoes in all seasons.

Shopping Tips

Shopping is an extremely popular activity in Boston, and most of the city's best shopping areas can be found featured in this guidebook. A fantastic variety of merchandise in every price range is available; most stores accept major credit cards; and there is no state sales tax on clothing, except for items of clothing retailing in excess of $175, when a 6.25 percent tax is charged on the amount over $175.

Back Bay offers two luxury shopping plazas: **Copley Place** *(see p74)* with 75 distinctive stores, including Neiman Marcus, Jimmy Choo, and Louis Vuitton; and the **Shops at Prudential Center** *(see p88)* featuring Saks Fifth Avenue and 70 more stores. Nearby **Newbury Street** *(see pp24–5)* is where the big-name fashion designers have shops, as well as high-end home furnishings, antiques and art galleries. Newbury Street shops get funkier toward Massachusetts Ave. One block away, Boylston Street has plenty of top sporting goods emporiums and famous-name chain stores.

Historic Beacon Hill is home to a cluster of exceptional antique shops along Charles Street *(see p75)* that are surrounded by exclusive little clothing and shoe boutiques. In studenty Cambridge, Harvard Square *(see p75)* is well known for its fine selection of bookstores, along with 150 boutique shops and chain stores concentrated in a small area. The carnival-like atmosphere of historic

Faneuil Hall Marketplace *(see p75)* creates a fun shopping experience, with its buskers, chain stores, and an eclectic collection of pushcart stalls offering high-quality souvenirs, handmade jewelry, local crafts, and clothing.

Truly unique gifts and souvenirs can be found in Boston's museum shops and gift stores at major attractions. Most of these shops carry high-quality, specialty items related to their collections, as well as popular lower-cost souvenirs. **The Museum of Fine Arts** *(see pp28–31)*, **Museum of Science** *(see pp16–17)*, and the **Isabella Stewart Gardner Museum** *(see pp34–5)* particularly merit a visit to their gift shop at the end of your visit. Also check out the specialty museums, such as the **USS Constitution Museum** *(see pp37)* and the **New England Aquarium** *(see pp38–9)*.

There are several large shopping malls located just outside the city. West of the city, **Chestnut Hill Mall** has Bloomingdales and 60 high-quality shops and boutiques. The huge **Burlington Mall**, north of the city, has Nordstrom, Macy's and almost 200 other popular stores. **Natick Mall** is the largest in New England with 300 upscale stores, and is anchored by Neiman Marcus, Nordstrom, and Macy's. There are two outlet malls, **Wrentham Village Premium Outlets** with 170 high-end brands, and the smaller **Outlets at Assembly Row** in Somerville, complete with dining, LEGOLAND Discovery Center and a waterfront park.

DIRECTORY

GENERAL INFORMATION

Boston National Historical Park Visitor Center
☎ 617 242 5642
🌐 nps.gov/bost

Cambridge Office of Tourism
☎ 617 441 2884
🌐 cambridgeusa.org

City of Boston Visitor and City Information
🌐 cityofboston.gov

Greater Boston Convention & Visitors Center
☎ 617 536 4100
🌐 bostonusa.com

Massachusetts Office of Travel & Tourism
☎ 617 973 8500
🌐 mass-vacation.com

DISABLED TRAVELERS

Greater Boston Convention & Visitors Center
🌐 bostonusa.com/visit/planyourtrip/getting around/accessiblity/

MBTA Office for Transportation Access (OTA)
🌐 mbta.com/riding_the_t/accessible_services

SHOPPING

Burlington Mall
🌐 simon.com/mall/burlington-mall

Chestnut Hill Mall
🌐 simon.com/mall/the-shops-at-chestnut-hill

Natick Mall
🌐 natickmall.com

Outlets at Assembly Row
🌐 assemblyrow.com

Wrentham Village Premium Outlets
🌐 premiumoutlets.com/outlet/wrentham-village

Trips and Tours

Several city trolley tours depart from the **Visitor Information Center on Boston Common** (see p142), including **Old Town Trolley Tours** which offers narrated sightseeing on board old-fashioned trolley buses as well as seasonal and themed tours (ghosts, chocolate, etc). These trolley tours permit re-boarding all day, making them easy transit to major sites.

Boston Harbor Cruises depart from Long Wharf and offer harbor and lighthouse tours as well as whale-watching tours. Sightseeing and sunset tours of the Charles River on small cruise boats depart from Cambridgeside Galleria. The vessels of choice for romantic wedding proposals are the two authentic Venetian gondolas moored at the Charles River Esplanade.

Boston Duck Tours, especially popular with families, use open-topped amphibious vehicles that both trundle through the streets and navigate the Charles River.

Enthusiastic volunteers share their love of the city on guided walks. Among the many tour options available are the Freedom Trail, Victorian Back Bay, Beacon Hill, North End, Literary Landmarks, and the Dark Side of Boston.

Knowledgeable **Boston National Historic Park** rangers run tours of the Freedom Trail (see pp12–13), the Black Heritage Trail (see 82), and the Charlestown Navy Yard (see pp36–7). Rangers at Frederick Law Olmsted's National Historic Site run tours of portions of the Emerald Necklace (see p19), as well as tours of the office and grounds by reservation.

The New England Aquarium (see pp38–9) runs whale-watching trips with trained marine biologists. Ships carrying around 200–400 passengers make the 3.5 to 5 hour round trip to the Stellwagen Bank whale feeding grounds. The tours run from April through October.

Visitors can sample the colorful flavors of Boston's ethnic neighborhoods on foodie tours. **Boston Food Tours'** Chinatown tour visits markets, a herbalist, and ends with fresh dim sum, while another offers tastings, tips, and insights on the lively Italian food markets, restaurants, and cuisine of the North End.

Cover ground quickly with **Urban Adventours** narrated bicycle tours that include an overview of city highlights plus a few places off the tourist trail – enjoy a ride along the banks of the Charles River, a sunset spin along the waterfront, or a fall foliage tour through the Emerald Necklace.

Movie buffs will enjoy a walk or bus ride to iconic Boston film and television locations in the company of **On Location Tours**.

Dining Tips

Boston restaurants span a diverse scene, ranging from expensive celebrity chef establishments downtown and in Back Bay, to the affordable eateries found near the universities. Great meals can be eaten in the city's many small, independent and often ethnic eateries: Italian in the North End, Asian in Chinatown and the Theater District, and creative contemporary dishes in the South End. And when the weather is warm, choose a sidewalk café along Newbury, or head to the Waterfront for clam chowder, oyster bars and ocean-fresh seafood.

Boston being a major fishing port, fresh seafood is plentiful. City favorites are the sweet-tasting, large-clawed American lobster, as well as young haddock or cod, known locally as scrod, and bluefish, a stronger-flavored fish. You'll need to know your seafood terminology, too – a quahog is a large clam, while prized local oysters are known as American bluepoints.

Check out the latest rave reviews in **Boston Magazine** and reserve online with **Open Table** up to two weeks ahead for popular restaurants, or check for cancellations by calling the restaurant the same day. Some seat guests in the order they arrive. Be prepared to arrive by 6pm or wait. Many restaurants are casual, reasonably priced and welcome families. Breakfast is generally served from 7–10am, lunch from 11:30am–2pm and dinner from 5:30–10pm. A 7 percent tax is added to the dining total in Boston and Cambridge, and tips of 15–20 percent of the dining amount are expected. Alcoholic drinks are available in many restaurants. The legal age for drinking alcohol is 21 years, and a photo ID may be requested from patrons of all ages.

Where to Stay

Boston hotels are expensive, especially those in central Boston, close to principal tourist attractions – namely Back Bay, Beacon Hill, Downtown, and the Financial District. Hotels and inns outside the city center are a better bargain. Travelers accustomed to large motel rooms may be surprised by the small dimensions of some rooms in older Boston hotels, especially those in the lower price range. European-style twin-bedded rooms are uncommon; most have two double beds or one king- or queen-size bed.

Rates vary with the season, and also on how full the property will be on a particular date. Rates are highest between May and October, and when special events are in progress. The **Boston CVB** offers a comprehensive list of hotels, but does not provide a reservation service. For the best rates, check with online services such as **Kayak** and **Expedia**, and then call the hotel to ask for their best rate and any special packages they may offer. Hotel tax in the Boston area is 14.45 percent, and room rates are usually quoted without tax included.

There are other options for lodging beyond hotels, and if you are willing to forego the amenities and services of large hotels, many of these options offer lower prices.

For bed-and-breakfast properties, many of which are in historic or character homes, and include a full breakfast and often Wi-Fi as well, contact the **Bed and Breakfast Agency of Boston**. Savings can be made in "efficiency" (self-catering) apartments or rooms. Furnished apartments and homes often provide more space and amenities at a lower price. They usually have a full kitchen but no housekeeping service and are often located in residential areas. They can usually be booked through the same agencies as bed-and-breakfast, or **Vacation Rentals** and **Vacation Rentals by Owner** are agencies with many self catering properties on their books.

Another budget option is **Airbnb**, which lists both furnished apartments and shared-living-space bedrooms within a private residence. Boston also has several **hostels**, often with a choice of en-suite or dorm accommodations, including smart, central **Hostelling International**. You can even stay overnight in a cabin on a tall ship moored in Boston Harbor with **Liberty Fleet**.

DIRECTORY

TRIPS AND TOURS

Bicycle Tours
🅦 urbanadventurs.com

Boston Duck tours
🅦 bostonducktours.com

Culinary Tours
🅦 bostonfoodtours.com

Movie Tours
🅦 onlocationtours.com/boston-tours/

National Park Service Tours
🅦 nps.gov/bost
🅦 nps.gov/frla

Trolley Tours
🅦 trolleytours.com/boston
🅦 bostonsupertours.com/upper-deck-trolley-tours/

Walking Tours
🅦 bostonbyfoot.com

Water Tours
🅦 bostongondolas.com
🅦 bostonharborcruises.com
🅦 charlesriverboat.com

Whale Watch Tours
🅦 neaq.org

DINING

Boston Magazine
🅦 bostonmagazine.com

Open Table
🅦 opentable.com

ACCOMMODATIONS

Airbnb
🅦 airbnb.com

Bed and Breakfast Agency of Boston
🅦 boston-bnbagency.com

Boston CVB
🅦 bostonusa.com

Expedia
🅦 expedia.com

Hostelling International
🅦 bostonhostel.org

Hostels
🅦 hostels.com

Kayak
🅦 Kayak.com

Liberty Fleet
🅦 libertyfleet.com/boston-tall-ship-overnights

Vacation Rentals
🅦 vacationrentals.com

Vacation Rentals by Owner
🅦 vrbo.com

Places to Stay

Luxury Hotels

Eliot Hotel
MAP J5 ▪ 370 Commonwealth Ave, 02215 ▪ 617 267 1607 ▪ www.eliothotel.com ▪ $$
Back Bay grace and charm characterize this late 19th-century landmark hotel. Visiting musicians and baseball teams alike enjoy the spacious suites. Uni (see p93), the ground-floor restaurant, is one of Boston's most acclaimed and provides room service for the Eliot's guests.

Langham, Boston
MAP Q3 ▪ 250 Franklin St, 02110 ▪ 617 451 1900 ▪ www.langham boston.com ▪ $$
The extremely posh Langham occupies a jewel of an Art Nouveau building, the former Federal Reserve bank in the heart of the Financial District. Spacious rooms feature modernized Second Empire decor with rich brocades.

Millennium Bostonian
MAP Q2 ▪ Faneuil Hall Marketplace, 02109 ▪ 617 523 3600 ▪ www. millenniumhotels.com ▪ $$
Rooms run the gamut from tiny to palatial in this elegant and swanky oasis close to bustling Faneuil Hall Marketplace (see p75 & p101), but all feature lovely city views. There is an excellent on-site fitness center.

Taj Boston
MAP M4 ▪ 15 Arlington St, 02116 ▪ 617 536 5700 ▪ www.tajhotels.com ▪ $$
The 1927 "original" Boston Ritz benefits from a great location on the edge of the Common and had a thorough restoration in 2002 to revive its old-fashioned glory. This grande dame epitomizes opulence, decorum, and "old Boston" style. The lobby bar is legendary.

Boston Harbor Hotel
MAP R3 ▪ 70 Rowes Wharf, 02110 ▪ 617 439 7000 ▪ www.bhh.com ▪ $$$
To enjoy one of the most beautiful locations in the city to the full, request a room with a harbor view and private balcony. There's no need to go anywhere else as you'll find restaurants, a fitness center, and spa all on site.

Four Seasons
MAP N4 ▪ 200 Boylston St, 02116 ▪ 617 338 4400 ▪ www.fourseasons.com ▪ $$$
Rock stars and visiting dignitaries often select the low-key luxury of this modern hotel on the edge of the Theater District. The lobby-level Bristol Lounge is a favorite spot for striking business deals, and the indoor pool is an added bonus.

Liberty Hotel
MAP F3 ▪ 215 Charles St, 02114 ▪ 617 224 4000 ▪ www.libertyhotel.com ▪ $$$
Dramatic design has transformed the historic Charles Street Jail into an elegant boutique hotel with a soaring lobby. Basketball and hockey teams stay here, as TD Garden is nearby.

Mandarin Oriental
MAP K6 ▪ 776 Boylston St, 02199 ▪ 866 526 6567 or 617 535 8888 ▪ www. mandarinoriental.com ▪ $$$
Situated in the heart of Back Bay, the Mandarin Oriental has some of the city's largest luxury rooms. The rooms come fitted with designer linens, huge bathtubs, and state-of-the-art electronics. Many guests stay on site to enjoy the full-service spa.

Revere Hotel
MAP N5 ▪ 200 Stuart Street, 02116 ▪ 617 428 1800 ▪ www.reverehotel. com ▪ $$$
This sleek, hip hotel is two blocks from Boston Common and close to the Theater District. Every elegant room has its own private balcony. There's a rooftop pool and bar, and fine Mediterranean dining in the Rustic Kitchen (host to The Cooking Show).

Ritz-Carlton, Boston Common
MAP N4 ▪ 10 Avery St, 02111 ▪ 617 574 7100 ▪ www.ritz-carlton.com ▪ $$$
This classy hotel is on the upper levels of the tallest

building overlooking the Common. Rooms are the height of contemporary elegance and offer a wealth of high-tech and luxury amenities. Guests can use the fitness center for a nominal charge.

XV Beacon

MAP P3 ■ 15 Beacon St, 02108 ■ 617 670 1500 ■ www.xvbeacon.com ■ $$$
The design-conscious decor and extraordinary attention to detail makes this chic but cozy boutique hotel in Beacon Hill a favorite with business executives. With just 60 rooms, all with high-tech extras, it is the most masculine of Boston's modern hotels.

Deluxe Hotels

Ames Hotel

MAP G3 ■ 1 Court St, 02108 ■ 617 979 8100 ■ www.ameshotel.com ■ $$
An elegant contemporary hotel, housed in a landmark building in the heart of downtown Boston, the Ames often has excellent weekend rates because it is mainly a business hotel. Suites retain their original fireplaces and windows with dramatic Romanesque arches. The contrasting minimalist room design tends toward the soothing rather than the stark.

Battery Wharf Hotel

MAP H2 ■ 3 Battery Wharf, 02109 ■ 617 994 9000 ■ www.battery wharfhotelboston.com ■ $$
Situated at the edge of the North End, this luxurious hotel commands the mouth of Boston Harbor. Guests benefit from a well-equipped fitness center and a luxury spa.

The Charles Hotel

MAP B2 ■ 1 Bennett St, Cambridge, 02138 ■ 617 864 1200 ■ www.charles hotel.com ■ $$
Extra touches, such as handmade quilts hanging on the walls, personalize the comfortable rooms at this modern hotel on the edge of Harvard Square. There's an indoor pool, an outstanding jazz club, the Reggattabar (see p128), and a top Boston restaurant, Rialto (see p66).

The Colonnade

MAP K6 ■ 120 Huntington Ave, 02116 ■ 617 424 7000 ■ www. colonnadehotel.com ■ $$
Often used by upscale tour groups, the Colonnade has some of the largest and most comfortable rooms in Back Bay, as well as the city's only outdoor rooftop pool.

Hotel Marlowe

MAP F2 ■ 25 Edwin H. Land Blvd, Cambridge, 02141 ■ 617 868 8000 ■ www.hotelmarlowe. com ■ $$
Located behind the Museum of Science, this sleek hotel creates a self-contained world of comfort with Internet access, evening wine receptions, and a fitness center. Check the website for last-minute deals.

Marriott Long Wharf

MAP R2 ■ 296 State St, 02109 ■ 617 227 0800 ■ www.marriottlong wharf.com ■ $$
The hotel's waterfront location means most of the bright, spacious rooms have superb harbor or city views. Waterline, the casual bar-restaurant, is the perfect spot for an evening cocktail.

Nine Zero

MAP G3–G4 ■ 90 Tremont St, 02108 ■ 617 722 5800 ■ www.ninezero hotel.com ■ $$
Nine Zero marries sleek and shiny steel, chrome, and glass with warm wood and designer furniture to achieve a contemporary look with a soft edge. Its location, on the Downtown Crossing corner of Boston Common, is very convenient.

Residence Inn Boston Back Bay / Fenway

MAP D5 ■ 125 Brookline Ave, 02215 ■ 617 236 8787 ■ www.residence innbackbay.com ■ $$
The Residence Inn is an upscale, contemporary extended-stay hotel that overlooks Fenway Park. Its suites offer separate living and dining areas and a full kitchen, plus amenities that include luxury bedding and free Wi-Fi. Guests can also take advantage of the complimentary breakfast and lounge. It's within walking distance of restaurants and shops.

Royal Sonesta

MAP F2 ■ 5 Cambridge Pkwy, Cambridge, 02142 ■ 617 806 4200 ■ www. sonesta.com ■ $$
An outstanding art collection, excellent restaurant, and a striking riverside location make this a top choice for aesthetes. Bargain summer family packages often available.

Seaport Hotel

1 Seaport Lane, 02210
■ 617 385 4000 ■ www.
seaporthotel.com ■ $$
Connected by a walkway
to the World Trade Center,
the Seaport was one of the
first to pioneer the South
Boston Waterfront. Rooms
are large and comfortable,
and the pool is a bonus,
as are regular shuttles
to Downtown.

The Verb Hotel

MAP D5 ■ 1271 Boylston
St, 02215 ■ 617 566 4500
■ www.theverbhotel.com
■ $$
In the shadow of Fenway
Park, this trendy, retro-
themed hotel is in demand
whenever there's a big
event around the corner.
The stylish atmosphere
attracts younger crowds
looking to celebrate.

Hip/Historic Stays

Boston Park Plaza

MAP M5 ■ 64 Arlington
St, 02116 ■ 617 426
2000 ■ www.bostonpark
plaza.com ■ $
The 1927 Park Plaza is
Boston's largest historic
hotel. Restoration has
thankfully put some
glamour back. Popular
with business travelers,
convention-goers, and
tour packagers, it is
convenient for Back Bay
and the Theater District.

Beacon Hill Hotel &
Bistro

MAP N3 ■ 25 Charles St,
02114 ■ 617 723 7575
■ www.beaconhill
hotel.com ■ $$
This town house hotel is
mere steps from Boston
Common. The rooms are
mostly small but Euro-
chic, and there's a first-
floor bistro that serves

breakfast (included in
rates). There's also a
roofdeck for guests.

The Boxer Boston

MAP P2 ■ 107 Merrimac
St, 02114 ■ 617 778 2900
■ www.theboxerboston.
com ■ $$
This stylish boutique hotel
offers rooms and suites
that show off a sleek,
"industrial chic" design
and are equipped with all
the latest amenities. It's
centrally located between
North End and Beacon
Hill, making it ideal for
exploring the city on foot.

Fairmont Copley
Plaza

MAP L5 ■ 138 St James
Ave, 02116 ■ 617 267 5300
■ www.fairmont.com ■ $$
This sister hotel of New
York's Plaza has been a
Copley Square landmark
since 1912. Public areas
are opulent, rooms are
small but comfy, and
suites are truly grand.

Gryphon House

MAP D5 ■ 9 Bay State Rd,
02215 ■ 617 375 9003
■ www.innboston.com
■ No DA ■ $$
This 1895 brownstone
town house boasts huge,
elegant rooms with fire-
places, wet bars, and high-
speed Internet. A quiet
spot, it is convenient for
Back Bay or the Fenway.

Hotel Commonwealth

MAP D5 ■ 500
Commonwealth Ave,
02215 ■ 617 933 5000
■ www.hotelcommon
wealth.com ■ $$
Right by Kenmore Square,
this suave 150-room hotel
has all the high-tech
essentials but with the
architecture and decor of
France's Second Empire.

Hotel Veritas

MAP C2 ■ 1 Remington
St, 02138 ■ 617 520 5000
■ www.thehotelveritas.
com ■ $$
This luxury four-story
boutique hotel near
Harvard University is
ideally situated for
families visiting students.
Combining luxury with
convenience, rooms in
this hotel are intimate
and contemporary,
while bathrooms have
marble finishes. A cozy
lounge in the lobby
serves cocktails.

Loewes Boston Hotel

MAP F5 ■ 350 Stuart St,
02116 ■ 617 266 7200
■ www.loeweshotels.
com/Boston ■ $$
This posh boutique hotel
in the handsome lime-
stone, former Boston
police headquarters
offers deluxe comfort and
services in a convenient
corner of South End.

W Hotel

MAP G5 ■ 100 Stuart St,
02116 ■ 617 261 8700
■ www.starwoodhotels.
com ■ $$
Seemingly designed as
much for the architectural
press as for the traveler,
this W appeals equally to
design mavens, and to
visitors who enjoy the
location in the Theater
District at the edge of
Back Bay. A Bliss Spa is
in the hotel.

Hotel
InterContinental

MAP H4 ■ 510 Atlantic
Ave, 02110 ■ 617 747
1000 ■ www.intercon
tinentalboston.com ■ $$$
This chic waterfront hotel
at the edge of Fort Point
Channel combines
sophisticated architecture

with luxurious decor of rich furnishings and textiles. Sumptuous bathrooms include a soaking tub as well as a walk-in shower.

Lenox Hotel

MAP L5 ■ 61 Exeter St, 02116 ■ 617 536 6300 ■ www.lenoxhotel.com ■ $$$

Known for exemplary service, luxurious modern comfort, historic elegance and eco-innovation, this Back Bay boutique hotel near Copley Square has served Boston visitors since 1900. Many of the spacious corner rooms have wood-burning fireplaces. Dine at the City Table, on New England seasonal fare, or at Sólás authentic Irish Pub.

Mid-Range Hotels

The Charlesmark

MAP L5 ■ 655 Boylston St, 02116 ■ 617 247 1212 ■ www.charlesmark hotel.com ■ $

Set in an 1892 Back Bay town house, the compact but ergonomic rooms of this boutique hotel feature custom-made woodwork, light-toned woodwork, and smart Italian tilework. Breakfast is included in the astonishingly low (for the area) rates.

Harborside Inn

MAP Q3 ■ 185 State St, 02109 ■ 617 723 7500, 888 723 7565 ■ www. harborsideinnboston. com ■ $

This modest boutique hotel is set in a historic (1858) spice warehouse. Rooms have wood floors, exposed brick walls, oriental rugs, and traditional furnishings.

Chandler Studios

MAP M6 ■ 54 Berkeley St, 02116 ■ 617 482 3450 ■ www.chandlerstudios boston.com ■ $$

This hip boutique hotel in a South End brownstone offers studios with ultra-modern furnishings, kitchenette and high-tech features. Check-in is via a keyless entry system. There's daily maid service but staff are not on-site.

Courtyard Boston Cambridge

MAP B3 ■ 777 Memorial Dr, Cambridge, 02139 ■ 617 492 7777 ■ www. marriott.com ■ $$

Large desks and great views are highlights of this older riverfront hotel. Amenities include a fitness center and a pool. The location isn't ideal unless you have a car.

Courtyard Boston Downtown

MAP N5 ■ 275 Tremont St, 02116 ■ 617 426 1400 ■ www.marriott.com ■ $$

At the edge of the Theater District, this 1920s tower hotel underwent restoration to give fresh glitter to its dramatic public spaces (think crystal chandeliers and marble columns). Rooms are small but modern with first-rate amenities.

Fairfield Inn & Suites Boston Cambridge

MAP F2 ■ 215 Monsignor O'Brien Hway, Cambridge, 02141 ■ 617 621 1999 ■ www.fairfieldboston cambridge. com ■ $$

This contemporary hotel is just across the Charles River from Downtown. Rooms features sleek design including an ergonomic workstation. There's

free Wi-Fi, free hot breakfast, and 24-hour fitness and business centers.

Inn at St Botolph

MAP E3 ■ 99 St Botolph St, 02116 ■ 617 236 8099 ■ www.innatstbotolph. com ■ $$

Great for a romantic getaway, this red-brick townhouse boutique hotel near Symphony Hall boasts the finest in contemporary design. The sunny rooms have queen-size beds.

Kendall Hotel

MAP E3 ■ 350 Main St, Cambridge, 02142 ■ 617 577 1300 ■ www. kendallhotel.com ■ $$

An artist-architect couple transformed this century-old Cambridge firehouse into a boutique hotel. The 77 rooms are decorated with firehouse memorabilia and antiques. Don't miss the Rooftop Retreat.

Sheraton Commander

MAP B1 ■ 16 Garden St, Cambridge, 02138 ■ 617 547 4800 ■ www.sheraton commander.com ■ $$

Harvard Square's original (1927) hotel has elegant, contemporary, decor. Some rooms are small, but public areas are pleasantly clubby, and the Cambridge Common location is enchanting.

Westin Boston Waterfront

MAP P4 ■ 425 Summer St, 02210 ■ 617 532 4600 ■ www.starwoodhotels. com ■ $$

Connected to the Boston Convention and Exhibition Center, this huge property serves business travelers well. Rooms offer great city views.

For a key to hotel price categories see p146

Bed-and-Breakfast

Beech Tree Inn
83 Longwood Ave, Brookline, 02446 ▪ 617 277 1620 ▪ www.thebeechtreeinn.com ▪ No DA ▪ $
Most rooms in this friendly Victorian-style B&B have private baths. Guests also have use of a parlor.

Bertram Inn
92 Sewall Ave, Brookline, 02446 ▪ 617 566 2234 ▪ www.bertraminn.com ▪ No DA ▪ $
In a quiet residential neighborhood, this B&B began life as a private, Tudor-Revival-style home. Its rooms and small suites are all tastefully decorated with styles varying between Arts & Crafts, late Victorian, and just downright eclectic.

A Friendly Inn at Harvard
MAP C1 ▪ 1673 Cambridge St, 02138 ▪ 617 547 7851 ▪ www.afinow.com ▪ $
This large Queen Anne-style house is steps from Harvard Square and the museums. The great location, gracious hospitality, and all mod cons, including Internet access, make this a very popular hotel, particularly with visiting scholars and prospective students.

Irving House
MAP C1 ▪ 24 Irving St, Cambridge, 02138 ▪ 617 547 4600 ▪ www.cambridgeinns.com ▪ $
An older rooming house turned B&B, Irving House is tucked away in a leafy neighborhood next to Harvard. Rooms vary from tiny to spacious and some share bathrooms.

Isaac Harding House
MAP C2 ▪ 288 Harvard St, Cambridge 02139 ▪ 617 876 2888 ▪ www.hardinghouse.com ▪ $
Situated in a quiet Cambridge neighborhood, this 1860s Victorian home is now a popular B&B. The 14 guest rooms are spacious and bright. High-speed Internet is available in public rooms.

John Jeffries House
MAP M2 ▪ 14 David G. Mugar Way, 02114 ▪ 617 367 1866 ▪ www.johnjeffrieshouse.com ▪ $
This former nurse's quarters now serves as a pleasant inn. Public areas sport the Neo-Federal look and there is a garden. The guest rooms are bare but cheerful, and most have kitchenettes.

Newbury Guest House
MAP K5 ▪ 261 Newbury St, 02116 ▪ 617 670 6000 ▪ www.newburyguesthouse.com ▪ $
Several Back Bay residences have been linked to create this homey 32-room guest house. Rooms vary in size, but tend to be cozy with eclectic furnishings. Good value for the location.

Oasis Guest House
22 Edgerly Rd, 02115 ▪ 617 267 2262 ▪ www.oasisgh.com ▪ $
Close to Berklee School of Music, the Hynes Convention Center, and Symphony Hall, Oasis has rooms in a town house on a quiet one-way street a little removed from the hubbub of Massachusetts Avenue. Guests can make use of a small, shared outdoor deck.

Aisling Bed & Breakfast
MAP F6 ▪ 21 E Concord St, 02118 ▪ 617 206 8049 ▪ www.aisling-boston.com ▪ $$
Housed in a 19th-century redbrick row-house on a tree-lined street in Boston's South End, this Victorian-style home features three comfortable en-suite guest rooms, central air conditioning and free Wi-Fi. A free hot and homemade breakfast is served in the dining room.

The Gilded Lily
MAP E6 ▪ 4 Claremont Park, 02118 ▪ 617 877 3676 ▪ www.thegildedlily-boston.com ▪ $$
On a quiet residential street in the South End two blocks from the subway, this Victorian home has been restored, modernized and attractively decorated. The two guest rooms, on the third and fourth floor, share a kitchen and have private bathrooms and free Wi-Fi. There is no elevator.

Clarendon Square Bed & Breakfast
MAP F6 ▪ 198 W Brookline St, 02118 ▪ 617 536 2229 ▪ www.clarendonsquare.com ▪ $$$
Comfortable, spacious, and sophisticated guest rooms and luxury suites are housed in a six-story South End Boston townhouse built in 1860. They offer designer fabrics, private bathrooms in limestone and marble, and the latest technology. Your luggage will be carried to and from your room for you as there is no elevator.

Budget Hotels, Inns, and Hostels

Boston Common Hotel

MAP F5 ▪ 40 Trinity Pl, 02116 ▪ 617 933 7700 ▪ www.bostoncommon hotel.com ▪ $

One of the best-kept secrets of Back Bay, this once-private club has cozy but comfortable rooms at relatively bargain rates. Some single rooms are available. There are good discounts in low season.

Chandler Inn

MAP M6 ▪ 26 Chandler St, 02116 ▪ 617 482 3450 ▪ www.chandlerinn.com ▪ No DA ▪ $

A popular choice for business travelers on a budget, this hotel in the South End is a short walk from Back Bay "T." Rooms are comfy with TVs and phones with voice mail.

College Club

MAP L4 ▪ 44 Commonwealth Ave, 02116 ▪ 617 536 9510 ▪ www.thecollegeclub ofboston.com ▪ No DA ▪ $

This private club, which is devoted to the promotion of higher education, also has guest rooms available in its sophisticated Back Bay town house. Several smaller rooms share bathrooms: these are only suitable for solo travelers.

Constitution Inn

MAP G2 ▪ 150 3rd Ave, Charlestown Navy Yard, Charlestown, 02129 ▪ 617 241 8400 ▪ www. constitutioninn.org ▪ $

This 147-room facility in Charlestown Navy Yard serves military personnel, but welcomes all. Rooms are clean and modern, and guests can use the fitness center with pool and sauna free of charge.

DoubleTree Club

Columbia Point, Dorchester ▪ 240 Mt Vernon St, 02125 ▪ 617 822 3600 ▪ www.double tree.hilton.com/Boston ▪ $

This recently renovated hotel is located near the HarborWalk and the John F. Kennedy Library and Museum. There's a free shuttle service to the airport and the Double-Tree Downtown hotel.

Hampton Inn

191 Monsignor O'Brien Hwy, Cambridge, 02141 ▪ 617 494 5300 ▪ www. hamptoninn.com ▪ $–$$

This chain hotel features high-speed Internet in all rooms as well as free underground parking. Rooms are modest but include a good-sized desk area, making it popular with business travelers on a limited budget.

Hostelling International

MAP P5 ▪ 19 Stuart St, 02116 ▪ 617 536 9455 ▪ www.bostonhostel. org ▪ $

Set downtown, a short walk from popular sights, this modern hostel offers single-sex dorms with bunk beds, or private en-suite rooms with TV. Continental breakfast is included, and a communal kitchen and laundry rooms are available.

Hotel 140

MAP F5 ▪ 140 Clarendon St, 02116 ▪ 617 585 5600 ▪ www.hotel140.com ▪ $

Just around the corner from the Back Bay Amtrak station, this budget hotel has refurbished the rooms of the country's first YMCA into neat examples of how best to use small spaces.

Hotel Tria

220 Alewife Brook Pkwy, Cambridge, 02138 ▪ 617 491 8000 ▪ www.hoteltria.com ▪ $

Situated near Alewife "T" station on the edge of Cambridge, the chic style and comfort of the Tria suggest luxury, but prices are within budget range.

Inn at Longwood Medical Center

342 Longwood Ave, 02115 ▪ 617 731 4700 ▪ www. innatlongwood.com ▪ $

This is an attractive, comfortable 144-room hotel in the Longwood Medical Area. Families of patients get the best rates but it is open to all travelers.

La Quinta Inn and Suites

23 Cummings St, Somerville, 02145 ▪ 617 625 5300 ▪ www.lq.com ▪ $

This motel is a four-minute walk from the MBTA Orange Line and offers an airport shuttle service. Spacious rooms and suites have tasteful decor and include cable TV, and high-speed Internet.

Holiday Inn Express

MAP F2 ▪ 250 Monsignor O'Brien Hwy, Cambridge, 02141 ▪ 617 577 7600 ▪ www.hiecambridge. com ▪ $$

This roadside Holiday Inn is geared to short-term business stays – the rooms have good work areas. There's limited free parking and it's a short walk to Lechmere "T" stop.

Boston

Acknowledgments

Author

Patricia Harris and David Lyon write about travel, food, fine arts, and popular culture for many publications including *Boston Magazine*, *Boston Globe*, *Yankee*, *Robb Report*, and hungrytravelers.com. They also co-wrote the Dorling Kindersley *Eyewitness Travel Guide to Boston*.

Jonathan Schultz is a travel writer based in Portland, Maine. He has contributed extensive local content to *Boston Magazine*, Boston. citysearch.com; LosAngeles.citysearch.com; as well as having compiled a guide to Boston for Z Publishing.

Additional contributor

Paul Franklin, Nancy Mikula

Publishing Director Georgina Dee

Publisher Vivien Antwi

Design Director Phil Ormerod

Editorial Michelle Crane, Rebecca Flynn, Rachel Fox, Fay Franklin, Freddie Marriage, Fíodhna Ní Ghríofa, Scarlett O'Hara, Sally Schafer

Design Richard Czapnik, Marisa Renzullo

Commissioned Photography John Coletti, Demetrio Carrasco, Rough Guides/Angus Osborn, Rough Guides/Susannah Sayler, Tony Souter, Linda Whitwam.

Picture Research Susie Peachey, Ellen Root, Lucy Sienkowska, Oran Tarjan

Cartography Subhashree Bharti, Suresh Kumar, James Macdonald, Simonetta Giori, Dominic Beddow

DTP Jason Little, George Nimmo

Production Linda Dare

Factchecker Pat Harris & David Lyon

Proofreader Kathryn Glendenning

Indexer Hilary Bird

Illustrator Lee Redmond

First edition created by Departure Lounge, London

Revisions Team

Hayley Maher, Ankita Sharma, Neil Simpson

Picture Credits

88b, 119bl; Marcio Silva 10bl, 13ca, 20cla, 103bl, 108h, 123cr; Peter Spirer 125cl; Woevale 112cla; Tsz Wai Wong 12cl; Jixue Yang 24bc, 56cl.

Fairmont Copley Plaza: Richard Mandelkorn 72b.
Fogg Art Museum: President and Fellows of Harvard College/Natalja Kent 21tc. **Freedom Trail Foundation:** 52cb.

Tres Gatos: 135cl. **Getty Images:** Boston Globe 48br, 60crb, 63tl, 66cb, 69br, 71bl, 75tr, 97cla, 111ca, 112br, 124tr, 126crb, /Ed Farrand 45cl; Kevork Djansezian 43clb; Steve Dunwell 118t, 132t; Eunice Harris 54br; Lou Jones 63crb, 107bc; Lonely Planet 10cl; Maremagnum 87tr; NBAE/Brian Babineau 77tr; Cindy Ord 73br; S. Greg Panosian 10crb; Greg Pease 58cl; Joe Robbins 117b; Stock Montage 44tc, Denis Jr. Tangney 43tl. **Greater Boston Convention & Visitors Bureau:** Boston Harbor Association 53cl; Leise Jones Photography 6tl. **Grill 23:** 93br.

Harvard Museum of Natural History: 20cb. **Harvest:** 67crb.

International Poster Gallery: 90c. **Isabella Stewart Gardner Museum:** 34cl, 34bl; *The Ascension of Christ* (15th century) Russian, Novogorod, Tempera on panel, 52 x 36 cm (20 1/2 x 14 3/16 in.) 11cb; Sienna Scarff 34-5; *Portrait of Isabella Stewart Gardner* (1888) by John Singer Sargent 35tl.

L.A. Burdick Chocolatiers: 71tr. **L'Espalier Restaurant:** 66cla. **Legal Sea Foods:** Gustav Hoiland 105tr; Heath Robbins 68cb. **Lekker Home:** 110tr. **David Lyon:** 120tr.

Magpie: Danielle Freiman 126ca. **The Middle East:** 128tl.

New England Aquarium: 38crb, 38bl, 38-9, 39tl. **Newbury Comics:** 91cl.

Peabody Museum of Archaeology & Ethnology Harvard University: President and Fellows of Harvard College 21bl.

Robert Harding Picture Library: Richard Cummins 4crb; Franz Marc Frei 4cr; James Kirkikis 4cla; Michael Neelon 36cla.

Sweet Cheeks Q: 121clb.

Tadpole: 110bl. **The Hawthorne:** Gustav Hoiland 120bl. **The Kirkland Tap & Trotter:** Michael Piazza 129clb. **The Sports Museum:** 48tl. **The Thinking Cup:** Bill Lyons 70t. **Top of the Hub Lounge:** 92t.

USS Constitution Museum: 37ca.

Cover

Front and spine - **Getty Images:** Huntstock.
Back - **Dreamstime.com:** Wangkun Jia.

Pull Out Map Cover
Getty Images: Huntstock.

All other images © Dorling Kindersley
For further information see: www.dkimages.com

*As a guide to abbreviations in visitor information blocks: **Adm** = admission charge; **D** = dinner; **L** = lunch.*

DK | Penguin Random House

Printed and bound in China

First American Edition, 2003
Published in the United States by
DK Publishing, 345 Hudson Street,
New York, New York 10014

Copyright 2013, 2016 © Dorling
Kindersley Limited

A Penguin Random House Company

16 17 18 19 10 9 8 7 6 5 4 3 2 1

Reprinted with revisions 2005, 2007, 2009, 2011, 2013, 2015, 2016

Published in Great Britain by Dorling Kindersley Limited.

A catalog record for this book is available from the Library of Congress.

ISSN 1479-344X
ISBN 978-1-4654-4577-3

MIX
Paper from responsible sources
FSC™ C018179

SPECIAL EDITIONS OF DK TRAVEL GUIDES

DK Travel Guides can be purchased in bulk quantities at discounted prices for use in promotions or as premiums. We are also able to offer special editions and personalized jackets, corporate imprints, and excerpts from all of our books, tailored specifically to meet your own needs.

To find out more, please contact:

in the US
specialsales@dk.com

in the UK
travelguides@uk.dk.com

in Canada
specialmarkets@dk.com

in Australia
penguincorporatesales@
penguinrandomhouse.com.au

Street Index